Sights and Scenes of the World

A HUNDRED YEARS AGO

SIGHTS AND SCENES OF THE WORLD.

A PHOTOGRAPHIC PORTFOLIO

OF THE

MARVELOUS WORKS OF GOD

AND THE

WONDERFUL ACCOMPLISHMENTS OF MAN.

.... EMBRACING A ....

RARE AND ELABORATE COLLECTION OF THE MOST BEAUTIFUL AND NOTED EXAMPLES OF PALACES, CASTLES, CATHEDRALS, PAINTINGS, LAKES AND PICTURESQUE SCENERY ON THE FACE OF THE GLOBE, INTERSPERSED WITH INSTANTANEOUS PHOTOGRAPHS OF STREET SCENES IN THE WORLD'S GREAT CITIES.

DESIGNED TO TAKE THE PLACE OF AN EXTENDED TOUR AROUND THE WORLD.

DESCRIPTIONS OF THE SCENES HAVE BEEN PREPARED BY AN EXTENSIVE CORPS OF DISTINGUISHED TOURISTS, THE WHOLE PRODUCED UNDER THE PERSONAL SUPERVISION OF THE EMINENT TRAVELER,

EDWARD L. RAYMOND.

CHICAGO,
W. B. CONKEY COMPANY,
PUBLISHERS,
1895.

This Edition
was adapted from the original book
AND PUBLISHED BY
The Peterhouse Press
BRILL · BUCKINGHAMSHIRE · ENGLAND
1992

This edition is published by The Peterhouse Press
and adapted from an original publication
by W. B. Conkey and Company, Publishers
Chicago, Illinois, U.S.A. in 1895.

Edited and adapted by Peter Medcalf
with technical assistance from
Avocet Typesetters, Bicester, Oxon, U.K.
who undertook the typesetting
and the reproduction and enhancement
of the original half-tone illustrations.

ISBN 0 946312 02 8

Printed by Avocet Press, Bicester, Oxon, U.K.

CONTENTS

THE STORY BEHIND THIS BOOK

A few years ago my wife and I were visiting a friend in Sherborne, Dorset and we spent some time browsing through the local bookshops, an activity of which I am particularly fond. On this occasion we came across the original of this book. From the outside it was a fairly typical book of travel pictures produced in Chicago in 1895 in a landscape format 10¾ inches by 13¼ inches (272 mm × 335 mm) quarter bound in leather. The binding was damaged but the inside of the book was in quite good order.

What was remarkable was that the illustrations were not engravings as most British books would have been at that time but a splendid collection of photographs from all over the world reproduced by the 'Half-tone' process which was very much in its infancy at that time having only become commercially practicable with Max Levy's invention of the precision cross ruled screen in Philadelphia in 1886. In spite of the low contrast of the originals, the poor paper and the use of a rather coarse screen I felt (being a printer by trade) that the pictures were capable of enhancement and could now with modern techniques and materials produce a unique record of the world as it was then. This has proved to be the case.

What made the book even more interesting was that the collector was a world traveller himself who had written or collected from others a two or three hundred word comment on each picture remarking not only on the visual impact of the scene, the architecture and so on but giving impressions of the life of the place and its people as observed by American travellers of the time.

Life has changed dramatically over the century that has passed since these pictures were taken and together with the comments they portray this vividly. The impact of the motor car, the aeroplane, and radio and television had yet to come as had two devastating World Wars. Strasbourg was then a German city and Carlsbad was noted as in Bohemia, not Czechoslovakia. Central Europe was dominated by Germany and Austria, the British and French colonial empires controlled a large proportion of the globe and the Ottoman and Russian Czarist Empires were still powerful forces. America was emerging as a world power but was only beginning to take a real interest in the world outside its own continent.

In spite of all this one of the most noticeable features of the pictures of the older cities is how little they have changed. Apart, that is, from the nature of the traffic in the streets which is shown as still predominantly horse drawn. The internal combustion powered automobile was only just then emerging from the experimental stage. Traffic aside, however, the views of London, Paris, Vienna etc. have changed hardly at all. Princes Street Edinburgh is a particularly good example of this as is London's Trafalgar Square. Berlin and Dresden are exceptions because of the wars and it is tragic to see what beautiful and distinguished urban scenes have been lost. It is good to have them recorded here. In new cities such as Auckland in New Zealand the roads often appear to be unpaved and it is strange to see New York without skyscrapers.

It appears that the Hawaiian Islands (then the Sandwich Islands) were in the observer's view licentious and dissolute and he remarks that this may be because there is no word for virtue in their native language. Drugs were not yet considered a problem, the traveller reporting on San Francisco is much more concerned about the social impact of alcohol and he remarks that opium in Chinatown was used 'in its place'.

The writers appear liberal for their time. At least one is very critical of the treatment of aborigines around the world and is not afraid to be, by implication, critical of his own nation's treatment of the American Indian. This does not stop another observer referring to 'darkies' in another context.

Throughout the book we find little gems of information: for example that Bombay passed to the English Crown as part of the dowry of 'Princess Catherine' (presumably Catherine of Braganza the wife of King Charles II) and that in Melbourne, Australia between the years 1837 and 1882 the cost of certain building plots rose from $170 to $200,000.

It has only been possible to include about two-thirds of the pictures from the original book. This is mainly to ensure that the extent and therefore the price of this edition is not too expensive but also because a number of the subjects are of rather specialised interest. This is particularly so in regard to those showing in detail the World Columbian Exposition which took place in Chicago in 1893 and which may well provide the basis for a separate book at some time in the future.

For technical reasons the pictures have been reduced in size in this edition and the use of a square format has allowed more space for the text which was barely legible in the original. The pictures and comment were also distributed through the original book in what appears to be a rather random manner. We have tried to place them in a more logical sequence and list them alphabetically under national headings as they existed at the time. This perhaps destroys some of the inconsequential charm of the original but should reduce frustration in the reader trying to find a particular entry which previously was a time consuming exercise.

In the original very small type (a small face of about 8pt.) was used over a line length of ten inches resulting in almost nil readability. The use of the new format has allowed the use of double column setting with some space between the lines and reading is now, we hope, not so difficult. The decorative initials have been retained.

Finally we should draw attention to the fact that in the original book there were a number of illustrations with flaws in them: sometimes through bad printing, sometimes because of marks sustained during use. In most cases these subjects have been retained 'warts and all' in order to make the book as complete as possible. The editor and publishers apologise for these, comparatively few, blemishes and hope that they will not detract too much from the reader's interest and enjoyment.

PETER MEDCALF 1992

A LIST OF THE PICTURES

INTRODUCTION.

TO KNOW one's country should be the first duty as it is the most enduring pleasure of man. To know all countries is to reach the highest state of intellectual development. How to obtain this knowledge has heretofore been a vital question. Our lives are but a brief space, and comparatively few have the means or the fortitude to travel from country to country, risking health and comfort, to inspect even a small portion of the wonderful things this great world has in store for us. The great mass of people must therefore depend upon books to take the place of travel. In the preparation of "Sights and Scenes of the World" the traveler and artist have penetrated foreign lands, and returning place before us exact counterparts of the mighty pyramids, the lofty cathedral, the awful cataract and other beauties of the world. As a result we may sit in comfort by our firesides and see pass before us in one grand panorama, England, Scotland, Ireland, France, Germany, Austria, Turkey, Italy, Spain, Asia, Africa and South America, the Old World and the New. We see spread before us an object lesson in history so simple a child may understand, and so intensely interesting that the old are held spellbound while passing from scene to scene.

To introduce Mr. Edward L. Raymond, under whose personal supervision this work has been produced, is entirely superfluous, as for twenty years his name has been a household word expressive of travel. His long and brilliant career has fitted him as is no other traveler fitted for preparing a work of this kind.

He has been an indefatigable traveler, a close observer and a brilliant scholar, whose long experience has taught him what will best instruct the mind and delight the eye. This extensive travel and study has enabled him to gather from the "World's Storehouse" the choicest treasures, the rarest gems of nature and of art. He has surveyed the entire world and selected for this great volume scenes surrounded with the romance and history of past ages; castles whose towering battlements centuries ago looked down on scenes of war, misery and barbaric splendor; cathedrals built by ambitious monarchs, every stone telling a story of ignorance and oppression; the homes of kings and queens, pretentious but unhappy rulers of the past and present; mountain scenes rivaling in glory the splendor of the sun itself; the tropics teeming with vegetable and animal life; the home of the Esquimaux and the Land of the Midnight Sun. He takes us in Bonnie Scotland to Burns' birthplace and the home of Walter Scott; in England to Stratford-on-Avon, where dwelt the great Shakespeare and his fair Ann Hathaway; Stoke Pogis Churchyard, the place in which was written Grey's Elegy In A Country Churchyard, to famous London Bridge, about which we used to sing when children, "London Bridge is falling down," the Tower of London, and the Old Curiosity Shop immortalized by Charles Dickens; in France to Paris and Versailles, where the mighty Napoleon planned the conquest of nations, and to Monte Carlo's famous gambling den; in Berlin to the very house where Bismarck, the Iron Chancellor, mourned for the return of past powers; in Rome to the Colosseum, where gladiators and wild beasts fought for life to please Nero and his savage followers; to the Orient where Cleopatra lured kings to death, and in Jerusalem to Bethlehem, the birthplace of the Saviour. He leads the way through the great galleries of Versailles, Luxembourg, Dresden, Florence and ancient Rome, showing the world's masterpieces in painting and statuary. In the New World he takes us step by step from Greenland and Alaska in the North to Patagonia in the South. In our own country he shows us all the principal sights, the splendor of the Sierras; in Mexico we visit the homes of the Montezumas and scenes made famous by the luckless Maximilian; and see as they are to-day, Brazil, Argentine Republic, and little but tempestuous Chili. Who would not enjoy a Tour of the World with such an accomplished companion and guide?

Millions of dollars are annually spent by tourists vainly endeavoring to see the treasures shown in this book. Many they never see, and those they do but few appreciate because they do not remember the history connected with them. In this work we not only see scenes true to life from every land, but are given in few words their entire description and history.

An unusual degree of care has been exercised by Mr. Raymond in selecting the photographs for this great work. Every phase of life is represented. He shows us remote corners of the Earth where the foot of white man seldom treads. The photographing of so many scenes in distant lands has cost thousands of dollars, but the result justifies the enormous expense and labor involved. Such a collection we here present to what we feel sure will be an appreciative public.

THE PUBLISHERS.

Above is a photographic reproduction of the original introduction in the 1895 book.

CAPE TOWN, AFRICA.—The here pictured city is the capital and seat of government of Cape Colony, and lies at the head of Table bay on the northern side of the peninsula formed by Table mountain, thirty miles north of the Cape of Good Hope. It was founded in 1652, and at first consisted of a few houses under the shelter of a fort. The chief streets of the town were laid out at right angles, but the outer streets and suburbs extend irregularly. The city is now paved and has all modern improvements. Its architecture generally retains the feature given to it by earlier settlers, the houses being of brick faced with stucco, with flat roofs; but these are lately giving place to edifices of more modern design. The scenery around the head of Table bay is very striking. Table mountain with its branches, the Dells Peak and the Lion's Head, rise in a massive wall immediately at the back of Cape Town. During the prevalence of souteast winds it was covered by a dense, white sheet-like cloud, as here pictured, partially overlapping its side like a table-cloth, which has given rise to the saying, when such is the condition, that "The table-cloth is now spread on Table mountain." Along the base of this mountain where lie the suburban villages, the land is covered with luxuriant vegetation and studded with villas. The summit of Table mountain is occasionally sprinkled with snow for a day or two.

THE POSTOFFICE, BUENOS AYRES.—Buenos Ayres, the capital of the Argentine Republic and of the province of Buenos Ayres, is situated on the right bank of the estuary of the La Plata. The river is at this point so wide that it is quite impossible, with the naked eye, to distinguish its opposite bank. The town of Buenos Ayres is situated in a vast plain extending westward to the Andes. The level uniformity of its outline is only broken by the spires of the various churches. The stranger, on landing, is struck with the regularity of the streets, which are quite straight, and intersect each other at distances of one hundred and fifty yards, forming squares like those of a chess-board, with the cleanly appearance of the houses and the general air of independence that distinguishes the inhabitants. One of the principal buildings in the city is the here photographed building. The Buenos Ayreans inherit from their ancestors much of that passion for music which characterizes the Spaniard. Poetry, also, is much cultivated among them. Buenos Ayres contains many literary and scientific institutions for the promotion of agriculture. The charitable societies, though not very numerous, are rather important.

THE STOCK EXCHANGE, BUENOS AYRES.—The Stock Exchange of Beunos Ayres is one of the most important edifices in the city. It is an imposing structure of brick, stone and mortar, after the renaissance style and covered, like most South American buldings, with stucco. The Bolsa of Buenos Ayres is not only a stock exchange; it plays the part of the Bourse of Paris, and is to that city what the clubs and hotel lobbies are to the citizens of the United States. The Bolsa is open from morning to night, although the hours from twelve to one, and from three to four are mainly occupied in the legitimate business of stocks, principally the gambling in gold; but between, after, and before those hours the Bolsa is the rendezvous of all the well-to-do men of the city; they lounge in the luxuriously furnished library and discuss the news and gossip of the day; one meets his friends, swaps cigarettes or Havana cigars, and talks of everything except, perhaps, stocks. "Let's go to the Bolsa" is the common invitation and means just what here signifies: "Let's go over to the club." The Bolsa was created in 1835 and had its first sessions in a circular hall then known as the foreigners' hall; in 1841 it was closed by President Rosas, who objected to the exclusion of the general public, and in 1854 it was thrown open to the public and has continued to be the center of trade in the city.

STREET SCENE IN MELBOURNE.—The land on which this city now stands was sold in allotments of one-half acre (equal to about five lots, twenty-five by one hundred and twenty-five feet in size) in 1837 for one hundred and seventy dollars each. In 1882 the same ground brought as high as two hundred thousand dollars, and at this date is worth probably half as much more. But though land has thus increased in value Melbourne is not a crowded city. The streets are all ninety-nine feet wide, and the parks, public grounds, etc., are so numerous that though with about one-twelfth of the population the city covers an area as large as London. The botanical gardens of Melbourne are of world-wide fame. There is no city where more has been done for the working classes, or where they have made so good use of their advantages. Many of their efforts at government (for they have all the power in their own hands) have been ill-advised, but individually they have exhibited a prudence of which the community reaps the fruits. It is one of the peculiarities of Melbourne that about three out of four of the mechanics who have reached middle life, own their own houses—the neat cottages which they occupy.

'CIRCULAR QUAY.' SYDNEY.

CIRCULAR QUAY, SYDNEY, AUSTRALIA.—The busy scene here pictured is that at one of the public docks in Sydney. Sydney's situation (on a piece of land so cut by water as to produce a water-front of nearly one hundred and twenty miles) is one of the chief causes of its having attained the proud position it has among maritime cities of the world. The port is flanked on both sides by a number of promontories, so that in addition to a broad central channel with deep water, there is a series of sheltered bays with good anchorage. The entrance is a mile wide with a minimum depth of water of fifteen fathoms. The water front of Sydney is divided between public and private owners, the government owning three docks or quays, such as here shown. Sydneyites are great people for owning suburban residences. The "400" reside almost enirely out of town—within easy distance, however, of the heart of the city. The aborigines of Australia have been treated about as have been our American Indians—their lands have been stolen from them without consideration. They are a race about as low as it has ever been civilization's fate to come in contact with, and they are rapidly fading from existence. Sydney's principal exports are mutton, hides, wool and similar products. Gold and silver are largely produced in Australia, the "Broken Hill" mine being a famous silver producer.

13

TOWN HALL AND CATHEDRAL, SYDNEY, AUSTRALIA.—Sydney has more the appearnace of one of the old European cities than any other Australian city. Some of the streets are narrow, while nearly all are irregular. In its lack of public spaces and spacious promenades it contrasts quite unfavorably with its sister towns. The town hall is one of the largest and finest buildings in Sydney. When in 1788 Captain Phillip arrived at Botany bay with a shipload of convicts, he found its flat shores unsuited for colonization, and was also deterred from locating there by the lack of fresh water, so Sydney was selected as the site for a city. Strange to say, the rejected site is now occupied by pumping works for supplying the city with fresh water. The metropolitan area of Sydney consists of a peninsula thirteen miles long, consisting alternately of bold cliffs and beautiful beaches. It occupies, therefore, a position enjoying singular natural advantages. The residents of Sydney are famous for their sporting proclivities. On Derby day there it is quite impossible to do any business, as everybody, from bootblack to merchant prince, attends the races. The abundance and cheapness of coal have combined to make Sydney a most important manufacturing center. The climate is mild and even, resembling closely that of the south of France.

IMPERIAL OPERA HOUSE, RINGE STRASSE, VIENNA.—This magnificent renaissance edifice was completed in 1869. The sumptuous decorations of the interior are by famous and well-known architects. Vienna was in mourning for many weeks after the 8th of December, 1881, for on that day five hundred and eighty persons lost their lives by the burning of the Ringe Theatre. This place of amusement was the second in the city, and situated a short distance down the street here shown. Offenbach's new opera was about to be presented, and some two thousand persons were present when the curtain rose; scarcely had the opera begun when it was discovered that the theatre was on fire. A fearful panic ensued many of the people in the galleries jumping to the floor below or crushing each other in their mad efforts to escape. In the midst of the confusion the gas meter in the basement exploded, leaving the building in total darkness, excepting where the flames were bursting forth. The room was filled with the fumes of gas, thus causing many to die of asphyxiation. In the upper galleries few escaped. Heaps of dead were found there by firemen and soldiers who had been called to the rescue. Hundreds who were carried out were badly injured, and not a few of them died. The calamity was one of the worst of the kind recorded in modern history.

PARLIAMENT BUILDING IN VIENNA.—This fine building was erected in 1883 at a cost of seven and one-half million dollars, and is lavishly enriched with statues. The visitor to Vienna would scarcely recognize the city now had he not seen it in thirty years. The changes that have taken place in Vienna since the completion of the "Ringe Strasse", on which this building is situated, has been well-nigh marvelous. The street which this building faces was formerly occupied by the fortifications which surrounded the city, but were leveled for the purpose of making a boulevard and enabling the city to grow beyond its then city limits. The traveler here beholds with marked admiration a series of imposing buildings, many of which are the finest in the world, which adjoin the parliament building here shown. The colossal statue shown on the top of the building represents "Victory" in chariots of bronze. The Historical Museum of the city of Vienna, the Exchange, the Hofburg Theatre, the Palace of Justice, the Natural History Museum, the Art Museum, the Library, Parliament House and other fine structures, all face this well-known Ringe Strasse. Within the last quarter of a century Vienna has acquired importance as a seat of art, of which nothing in its previous history gave promise. The city is justly famous for the beauty of its women, and Vienna styles are famous the world over.

16

THE BOURSE, OR NEW EXCHANGE, BRUSSELS.—The vast proportions and almost excessive richness of ornamentation combine to make this building worthy of being the commercial center at the important metropolis in which it is located. The principal front is embellished with a Corinthian colonnade, to which a flight of twenty steps ascend. The principal hall, unlike that of most of its kind, is cruciform in shape and covered with a dome about one hundred and fifty feet high in the center, borne by twenty-eight columns. Two fine marble staircases ascend to the gallery, which afford a survey of the principal hall; the cost of the whole structure amounted to eight hundred thousand dollars. A characteristic scene in Brussels is that of the central market, a covered provision hall resembling its namesake at Paris but on a much smaller scale. It contains the city meat, poultry, vegetable and fish market. At one end of the fish market the baskets of fresh fish arriving from the sea are sold by auction to retail dealers, who occasionally use a curious mixture of French and Flemish. Every fish auction is held under the supervision of the municipal authorities; the principal sales take place on Wednesdays and Fridays. The auctioneer commences with high prices for each lot and then gradually descends the scale until a bidder calls "myn", and thus becomes the purchaser.

PALACE OF JUSTICE, OR COURT HOUSE IN BRUSSELS.—This edifice, designed on a most ambitious scale and begun in 1866, was formally inaugurated in 1883 at a jubilee of Belgium's existence as a separate kingdom. The cost of the building amounted to ten million dollars. It is the largest municipal building of the present century and is certainly the most remarkable and one of the most beautiful of modern structures. The sub-structure rendered necessary by the inequalities of the site (it being built on the side of a hill) added greatly to the magnitude of the task. The area occupied by the building amounts to two hundred and seventy thousand square feet, which considerably exceeds that of St. Peter's at Rome, which is two hundred and twelve thousand square feet (the Cologne cathedral occupying eighty-seven thousand and St. Paul's in London one hundred and nine thousand square feet). The huge and massive pile stands upon an almost square base five hundred and ninety by five hundred and sixty feet, and forcibly suggests the mighty structures of ancient Egypt of Assyria. Indeed the architect avowed that his guiding principle was an adaptation of Assyrian forms to suit the requirements of the present day. The general architectural scheme may be described as pyramidal, each successive section diminishing in bulk. The gilt cross on the top of the dome is four hundred feet above the pavement.

18

CARLSBAD, THE FAMOUS BOHEMIAN WATERING PLACE.–Carlsbad receives annually upward of twenty-five thousand visitors. Its waters are especially efficacious in liver complaints. The town is situated in the narrow valley of the River Tepl, which is shown in this photograph. The pine-clad slopes of the hills are traversed by paths in all directions. The springs are said to have been discovered in 1347 by Emperor Charles IV, while hunting, but Carlsbad was known as a health resort a century earlier. The oldest and most copious of the springs is the Sprudel, on the right bank of the river, which yields about thirty-three cubic feet per minute. The Sprudel colonnade, an imposing iron structure which is seen in the center of this picture, covers the spring, which gushes up in jets one and a half feet thick of from forty to sixty per minute, and varying from six to thirteen feet in height. One peculiarity of this watering place is that the town owns the springs, and all comers are taxed by what is known as a "visitor's tax" for those who stay a week or more no charge being made for drinking the water at the springs. They have a peculiar way of dividing visitors into classes and taxing accordingly. The first class pays five dollars, the second three dollars and the third two dollars, in addition to which there is a music tax for each family during the summer, ranging from $8.50, 1st class, to $1.00, 3d class.

THE CITY OF MONTREAL, CANADA.—Montreal is a reflection of Canada. Here is the old Canada side by side with the new, with a quarter of million inhabitants, at the head of ocean navigation, yet in the heart of this vast continent and with all the reserves of the Northwest seeking an outlet from her port. Montreal is the commercial metropolis of Canada, and a city with the securest possible future. The city takes her name from the mountain which stands guard over her. In a succession of terraces the streets climb the mountain, the summit of which is reserved to the citizens as a matchless park. In the foreground of this picture the two spires shown are those of the Church of Notre Dame, one of the largest ecclesiastical structures on the American continent. It can easily accommodate fifteen thousand people within its walls. Its towers are two hundred and twenty-seven feet high, and one of them contains the largest bell in America, which weighs twenty-nine thousand four hundred pounds. From the summit of the tower a splendid view of the city and its environs is to be obtained. The cost of the building exceeded six million dollars. Alongside of Notre Dame stands the ancient seminary of St. Sulpice, which was built more than two centuries ago, its massive walls pierced with loopholes looking grimly down on the thronged yet peaceful street.

THE PARLIAMENT BUILDINGS, OTTAWA, CANADA.—These parliament buildings are designed in modified twelfth century Gothic style of architecture and are an admirable combination of simplicity, grace and strength. This building stands at the back of a spacious square and occupies a stone terrace with broad, sloping approaches. It is surmounted by a well proportioned tower two hundred and twenty feet in height. The generally accepted best view of the building is that standpoint from which this photograph is taken. From a number of points of view the buildings present a combination in a way that gives the keenest pleasure to the eye. The first stone of the building was laid by the prince of Wales on his visit to America in 1860, and in their present form they have cost about five million dollars. Ottawa contains other fine buildings, among which may be mentioned the post office, the great Roman Catholic cathedral, and other prominent structures, but they are so entirely overshadowed by the noble structures on Parliament hill that they are but little known outside of the city in which they are located. The season at Ottawa is during the winter months when parliament is in session, and then the ample grounds that surround the residence of the governor general become the scene of typical Canadian merry-making.

21

THE CITY OF QUEBEC, CANADA.—Among the cities of the New World, the grandest for situation, the most romantic in association, the most distinctive and picturesque in detail is the here pictured sentinel city that keeps the gates of the St. Lawrence river. Nothing could be more impressive than the view of the city of Quebec, taken from the same standpoint from which this photograph is taken, unless it is the matchless panorama, which is to be seen from the heights of the city looking up the river toward, or looking down the river from Quebec; it is hard to say which is the more impressive. The picture is one whose sublime lines and masses are brought out in full by the fresh coloring that plays over it. A famous French bishop asserted that only Heidelberg in Germany, Sterling and Edinburgh in Scotland, or Ehrenbreitstein in Germany can compare with Quebec for grandeur of situation and noblest beauty. The vast promontory which the city occupies is called Cape Diamond, so named from the numberless quartz crystals which once glittered over its surface. The French explorer, Jaques Cartier, visited the site in 1535 and repaid the hospitality with which he was entertained by the Indians by capturing their head chief and several others of the tribe, and taking them to France with him as trophies of his visit. When he returned the hostility of the Indians prevented an attempt to colonize the place.

HOUSES OF CONGRESS, SANTIAGO, CHILI.—"Congress House", or, the Cámara de Diputados, delegate chamber, in Santiago, Chili, is in the renaissance sytle, executed from a design by an Italian artist named Joaquin Tosca. Like most South American buildings, it is of brick covered with rose-colored terra-cotta stucco, and painted. The chamber is well furnished and presents a fine appearance when filled with the members of congress, who, for the most part, are the best educated and polished men of the republic. Much attention is given to education in Chili; the school budget for 1892 exceeded eight million Chilian dollars. English and American teachers are employed; the English language is most popular and considered of more importance than any other foreign language. It is also the fashionable society language of Chili. America came very near being embroiled in a war with Chili quite recently, which trouble was avoided only by the payment of $75,000 to the injured and heirs of the killed of the members of the crew of a United States vessel, who were attacked by a Valparaiso mob. The government of Chili is a republic modeled after that of the United States.

23

RAILROAD STATION, SANTIAGO, CHILI.—Santiago, the capital and most important city of the republic of Chili, is most picturesquely situated at the foot of the Andes, which not only make an imposing background, but render the climate most agreeable by protecting the city from the full force of the wintry blasts of the snow-capped peaks during winter and gently wafting those very breezes in the summer, which moderate the heat and make Santiago's one of the most delightful climates in the world. Santiago boasts of a fine theatre, subsidized by the government, and has its opera season in the winter; but the favorite resort of amusement is Santa Lucia, perched on the top of a hill, commanding a magnificent view of the city and of the surrounding country, and with the towering Andes as a background. Built inthe mediaeval style, Santa Lucia, from its battlemented towers, smiles upon the city extended at its feet, and nightly wafts through its portholes the light, graceful and, often, sensuous music of the Sanish zarzuela, or that of the frivolous French opera bouffe. The Alameda, or public promenade, of Santiago is magnificent avenue planted with fine trees and ornamented with statues, among which is that of General San Martin, whose march across the Andes is a historical feat not excelled by Hannibal and Napoleon.

TREASURY BUILDING, SANTIAGO, CHILI.—The Treasury Building, one of the most imposing edifices in Santiago, faces, like the majority of the most important buildings, on the Plaza Mayor. The plaza is beautifully and artistically laid out and has in the center a marble fountain, the central figure of which is a female symbolizing America, and receiving a baptism of the fire of independence. On the north is a beautiful edifice, two stories high, once the audiencia, or council chamber, but now used as offices of the intendant and the municipality. To the south and east are private buildings two stories high, stores, etc., etc. On the east is the old monastery, erected in the latter part of the seventeenth century by the Jesuit fathers, and destroyed twice by fire; once in 1841, and again on December 8, 1863, when two thousand persons, mostly women, were burned to death in the church. In the cloisters of the ruined church and monastery a magnificent edifice has been erected by the government as a National Institute, the first literary institution ever founded by the Chilian republic.

ENGLISH PARADE, HONG KONG, CHINA.–This remarkable city in China is the most typical of Chinese cities in those portions of it where English influence has not been felt and the construction of modern buildings not carried out. In regard to the every-day manners and customs of Chinese, it is strange to find how diametrically they are opposed to what we are familiar with. In a country where the roses have no fragrance, where the laborer has no Sabbath and the magistrate no sense of honor, where the needle of the compass points to the south, where the place of honor is on the left hand and the seat of intellect is the stomach, where to take off your hat is an insolent gesture and to wear white garments is to put yourself into mourning, it would seem useless to seek for any point of similarity with ours. The over-populated condition in which China has been for so many centuries has had a powerful influence in molding the national character. Vast as China is it cannot contain all those who call themselves her sons and daughters, and in many cities large sections of the inhabitants are driven to live in boats on the neighboring rivers and lakes. It is very difficult to see how the boat population provide food for those in their families. Indeed, were it not for the extreme cheapness of their daily food and their sober habits, they could not do so. Liquors appear to have no great attraction to Chinamen.

FRELSORS KIRK, OR, CHURCH OF OUR REDEEMER, COPENHAGEN, DENMARK.—A short distance from the busy center of Copenhagen is the here pictured church, the most remarkable feature of which is the steeple, with a stairway of three hundred and ninety-seven steps, built around the outside of it. A grand view of the coast of Sweden can be secured from its top. Copenhagen was founded in the twelfth century by Axel, bishop of Roeskilde, onthe site of a fishing village mentioned as early as 1043 (whence its original name Axelhus), and increased so rapidly through its trade that King Christopher, the Bavarian, made it his capital and residence in 1443. Christian IV, the most popular of the Danish kings, renowned not only as a warrior, but also as a wise ruler and a patron of industry and commerce, of science and art, greatly extended the town, chiefly by founding the Christianshavn quarter on the island of Amager, in which quarter the here pictured church is. In his reign the once strong fortifications were built, which successfully defied Charles X of Sweden in 1658 and 1659, and the united British, Dutch and Swedish fleets in 1700. The development of the city was powerfully influenced by the so-called Royal law of 1665, by which the Danish people and clergy, jealous of the power of the nobility, conferred absolute sovereignty upon King Frederick III. Thenceforeward Copenhagen became more and more distinctly the material and intellectual center of the nation, which prestige it retains to this day.

27

THE NATIONAL THEATRE, COPENHAGEN, DENMARK.—The here photographed theatre is one that any city might be proud to possess, not only for its beauty but for the associations which are connected with it. To the right and left of the entrance are bronze statues of the Danish poets Holberg and Oehlenschlager. Ludwig Holberg, born at Bergen, in Norway, is the founder of Danish comedy, but the statue on the other side of the entrance perpetuates the memory of Adam Oehlenschlager, who was a Copenhagen professor and the founder of Danish drama, he being the greatest of Danish dramatists. Adjoining the theatre, on its north, is the Copenhagen gallery, containing a most excellent collection of paintings, now numbering eight hundred and fifty in all, among which are three hundred and ninety-five by old masters, sixty-four by unknown and the rest by modern artists. The name of Copenhagen is derived from a Danish word meaning "merchants' harbor". It is the capital of the kingdom of Denmark and the residence of the king. It lies on both sides of the Kallebodstrand, a narrow and deep straight of the Sound which separates Zeeland from the small island of Amager. This strait forms the excellent harbor, to which the city is indebted for its early prosperity in trade. The commercial harbor is separated from the war harbor by a palisade intersecting the river. Down to 1870 the city was fortified on the side next the sea only, but fortifications are now being constructed on the landward side also. Several of the art and science collections of Copenhagen are of the highest rank.

FREDERIKSBORG PALACE, DENMARK.—The capital of the district of Frederiksborg lies at the south end of the small lake of Frederiksborg, from which, near the west bank, rises the here photographed palace. This palace was erected in 1602–20 by Christian IV, in a plain and vigorous renaissance style, on the site of an older building of Frederick II. The massive edifice, which consists of four stories, with towers and gables, has been restored since a fire in 1859, and is now fitted up as a historical museum. Some of the rooms are sumptuously decorated, especially the knight's hall and the dining-room. They contain a large collection of historic and artistic interest, modern historical pictures, portraits, etc. The windows afford a variety of pretty views. The palace church, the steeple of which can be seen rising just back of the palace, is where the kings of the Oldenburg line used to be crowned and is gorgeously decorated and almost overladen with gilding. The intarsia, or inlaid-work of the stalls next to the royal seat, dating from the time of Christian IV, is by Dutch artists; so, too, are the pulpit of ebony and embossed silver, and the Crucifixion in embossed silver over the king's oratory. The oratory, restored since the fire of 1859, is adorned with carvings in wood and ivory, and with fine paintings from the Passion by Prof. C. Bloch, presented by Herr J.C. Jacobsen. The park behind the palace, laid out in the old French style, contains the Slotspavilion, a restaurant, whence there is a fine view of the palace.

THE CITY OF ALEXANDRIA, EGYPT.—Alexandria was founded by Alexander the Great, the conqueror whose name it bears, who hoped thereby to consolidate Europe and India and make Alexandria the emporium of the world. The plan for the city was drawn by the same architect who built the famous temple of Ephesus, and is said to have resembled a Macedonian mantle in plan, intersected by spacious streets. Its temples and public buildings occupied one-fourth of the area, as every succeeding king added something to what already existed. Under the Caesars it was a world-renowned city, adorned with the arts of Greece and the wealth of Europe. Its school of learning outshone all those of the more ancient cities. At the commencement of the third century it began to wane; constant conflicts arising, sometimes from political and sometimes from religious causes, gradually brought about its ruin, but it must still have been a wonderful place when taken by Omar after a siege of fourteen months in 1641. From this date its commerce and importance sank rapidly, and the discovery of the route to India by the Cape of Good Hope completed its ruin. In the early part of the century Alexandria and its neighborhood was the scene of a bitter conflict between France and England for supremacy in the East. The city must ever remain the most commodious and the natural commercial emporium of Egypt.

THE PALACE OF GEZIREH, CAIRO.—The palace here pictured, which is internally a sumptuous edifice, was erected (after many interruptions and alterations) by a German architect in 1863, and it was the mansion in which guests who were invited to attend the ceremony of the opening of the Suez canal were entertained. The palace became state property in 1880, and is now seldom occupied. The masonry was executed by native workmen, the woodwork done in Vienna, and the marble work, which is most magnificent, done in Carrara, Italy. The principal apartments were designed by a famous interior decorator, and the silk hangings made by a Lyons silk manufacturer from designs that were drawn solely for that purpose. The furniture in a portion of the palace is Parisian; the balance was manufactured by a Berlin firm. The wings are surrounded by beautiful gardens, and contain suites of apartments for visitors, each of which consists of bedroom, dressing-room and sitting room. The upper floors contain similar apartments one suite of which was lined with blue satin when occupied by the unfortunate Empress Eugenie, wife of Napoleon III; and the middle apartment was fitted up for the reception of the Prince and Princess of Wales. The street scenes in the city of Cairo afford an inexhaustible fund of amusement and delight admirably illustrating the world of oriental fiction, and create an idelible impression on travelers.

PORT SAID.—The town of Port Said owes its origin to the Suez canal, and is the official residence of the general manager of the canal, which the city adjoins. To protect Port Said harbor from the deposits of mud which are washed to it from the Nile, enormous concrete docks over a mile in length were constructed at a prodigious cost. It was expected that Port Said would become a very large city and the prosperity of the place would increase rapidly, but its progress has been quite gradual, all Suez traffic going through instead of stopping at the entrance to the canal. The harbor proper consists of three principal sheltered basins, in which vessels discharge and load. The "Bassin Cherif", or chief basin, is flanked with the handsome buildings here shown, which were erected by Prince Henry, of the Netherlands, as a depot for facilitating the Dutch passenger and freight traffic between Europe and the colonies of Holland. On his death, however, they were purchased by the English government, and they are now used as a military depot and barracks. The town was named after Said Pasha, Viceroy of Egypt, without whose assistance at a critical period it is much questioned whether the Suez canal would not have been as great a fiasco as has the Panama canal.

THE SUEZ CANAL.—In 1854 De Lesseps, having matured his plan of the Suez canal, laid it before Said Pasha, who was then Viceroy of Egypt. He at once determined to carry out De Lesseps' plan. Difficulties wsere thrown in the way of the enterprise by the English government, but in 1856 permission to begin the work was granted by the viceroy. A considerable time elapsed before the necessary capital was raised and the work actually begun. The viceroy undertook to pay many of the current expenses, and provided twenty-five thousand workmen. In order to supply these workmen with water, four thousand water casks suitable for being carried by camels had to be constructed, and sixteen hundred of these animals were daily employed in conveying the workmen their supplies at a cost of sixteen hundred dollars a day. In 1863 a fresh water canal was completed, so that the company was thenceforth relieved of the enormous expense of furnishing water. In March, 1869, the water of the Mediterranean was at length allowed to flow into the canal. The first meeting of the waters of the two seas was by no means of an amicable character; they met boisterously and then recoiled from the attack, but soon, as if commanded by Father Neptune, they peacefully mixed. The picture here shown is one of the Suez stations with a party of travelers about to embark on the steamer.

BANK OF ENGLAND.—On Thread-needle street facing the Royal Exchange and the Mansion House stands the here pictured world-renowned Bank of England. It is an irregular building one story in height, the external walls of which are entirely devoid of windows, the bank being for the sake of security lighted from interior courts. The bank covers an entire block of four acres in extent. It was founded in 1691 by a Scotchman, who left as a legacy a law that no Scotchman should ever be permitted to act as one of the bank directors. Contrary to the usual belief, it is not a national, but a private institution, and was the first of the kind established in Great Britain. It is still the only bank in London which has the power of issuing paper money. Its original capital was six million dollars, which has since been multiplied more than twelve times. It employs over nine hundred people and manages the national debt, for which it receives an annual compensation of one million dollars, besides which it carries on the business of receiving deposits, discounting notes and lending money on other securities. The average amount of money negotiated at the bank per day is over ten million dollars. The bank's stationery, paper and printing of the bank notes are all done within its walls.

THE BANQUETING HOUSE, WHITEHALL, LONDON.—The above view represents one of the most interesting and historical localities in the metropolis. Macaulay describes it as "the most celebrated palace in which the sovereigns of England have ever dwelt." On the left is shown the old Banqueting Hall which is all that remains of Whitehall Palace. After the fall of Wolsey, in 1529, this property came into the hands of Henry VIII, who was so pleased with it that he changed its name from York Place and made it his own residence. Here, he married Anne Boleyn. The Banqueting House was built by Inigo Jones for James I, and is justly regarded as one of the finest and most remarkable edifices in London. In it, at one time, Charles I had a collection of 460 of the finest masterpieces of art, most of which were seized, sold or burned during the Reformation. In front of the Banqueting House, and facing the present Horse Guards, Charles I was beheaded, a passage being broken though the wall from which he stepped upon the scaffold. His statue now marks the spot where the execution took place. Oliver Cromwell was the next tenant of Whitehall, and died there in 1658. Looking down the street we see in the distance the towers of Westminster Abbey and the Houses of Parliament, while opposite is located the headquarters of the Horse Guards, beyond which stretches St. James Park and the old tilt-yard which is memorable as the scene of many of the pageants and tournaments of the courts of Henry and Elizabeth.

CHEAPSIDE, LONDON.—This street, which is one of the busiest in the city and rich in historical reminiscences, is now lined with handsome retail stores. Its jewelers and dry goods dealers have been famous from a time even earlier than that of honest John Gilpin, under whose famous race "the stones rattled as if Cheapside were mad." In olden times the neighborhood was frequently the scene of conflicts between the blood-thirsty and turbulent apprentices of the various rival "guilds" of trades unions. To the right and left diverge several cross streets, the names of which probably preserve the location of the different tradespeople in the far back period when Cheapside was an open market. Between Friday street and Bread street on the right once stood the Mermaid tavern, rendered famous as being the place of social gathering of Shakespeare, Ben Johnson and others. John Milton, the author of "Paradise Lost", was born in Bread street. One end of Cheapside leads into Mansion House Place and the Bank of England, while at the other end is found St. Paul's Cathedral and Ludgate Hill. Being such a direct thoroughfare, the traffic is sometimes so great that it is almost impossible for pedestrians to cross the street except at extreme risk.

CRYSTAL PALACE, LONDON.—On fine days nothing can be more delightful than a stroll through the grounds of the great Crystal Palace. It is situated upon a height commanding magnificent views of the surrounding scenery for many miles and is one of the best and cheapest, as well as the most prominent of London's many places of amusement. Here there is ample space for amusements and comfort in all kinds of weather and it is not unusual for 60,000 to 80,000 people to find amusement in this Palace in a single day. This vast structure was built in 1853 at the cost of nearly a million and a half pounds. Many of the materials which were used in its construction were taken from the great exhibtion in 1851. The length of the present building is 1,608 feet, with two aisles and transepts. The central transept is 390 feet long and the south transept is 312 feet long. The towers are 282 feet high and from them can be obtained a view which is well worth the fatigue of ascent. Within the building and in various parts of the grounds may be found thousands of objects of interest and the exhibitions, which are constantly being changed, provide ample amusement for persons of all tastes and ages.

THE THAMES EMBANKMENT, LONDON.–It hardly seems possible in looking at the above picture to consider that such a garden spot exists almost in the center of the great city of London. Only a few years ago the banks of the Thames were covered with buildings of very poor character. The above view shows the result of engineering works which have transformed these hovels into a paradise. One feature of London, which is often noticed, is the abruptness in which one may be transferred from busy and noisy thoroughfares to quiet courts and garden spots. Only a few steps from the scene above is the Strand, with its ever changing procession of humanity. The large building on the left as seen above, is Somerset House, which is now used for the Inland Revenue and other government offices. The tall obelisk in the center is one of Cleopatra's needles which was transported here some years ago from Egypt, its companion being now in New York City. On the right, in the distance, appears the tower of St. Paul's Cathedral and in front of it may be seen the outlines of Waterloo Bridge.

HYDE PARK CORNER, LONDON.—This is one of the most frequented and lively scenes in London. The park itself is surrounded by a handsome and lofty iron railing provided with numerous carriage-entrances, besides a great number of gates for pedestrians, all of which are shut at midnight. The entrance most used is that at Hyde Park corner. The handsome gateway at this corner, which is here pictured with three passages, was built in 1828; in the relief at the top are copies of the famous Elgin marbles which were executed by Phidias, the eminent Greek sculptor, to adorn the Parthenon at Athens, and are considered the finest specimens of the plastic art in existence. The originals are now in the British Museum. The first house to the right, adjoining Hyde Park gate, is the residence of the Duke of Wellington and was purchased in 1820 by the British government and presented to the duke as part of the nation's reward for his distinguished services on the field of Waterloo. The house next to it is the London residence of Baron Rothschild, the famous banker.

OXFORD STREET, LONDON.—This street is the principal artery of traffic between the populous northwestern quarter of the city and the business center, and extends a distance of one and a half miles. Along the eastern portion it contains a number of the most important retail stores in London, and presents the here pictured scene of immense traffic and activity. London, the capital of Great Britain, is also the metropolis of the civilized world, being not only the largest city, but the richest. With very nearly five million inhabitants, which eight hundred thousand houses suffice to shelter. It covers a territory twelve miles long and eight wide of costly buildings, and day by day the suburbs are being drawn into the huge vortex of the city. The "City of London" proper is but a small portion of the great metropolis, and may be fitly termed its counting house, being in reality the world's financial center. To the stranger, if he goes from America, London presents, from October to April, a cloudy, sombre hue, giving to the heart of the wayfarer a chilly and depressed feeling; but in those smoke-besmeared houses, the threshold once passed, are to be found the homes of true-hearted men and women. Without the glitter and glare of Paris, in their homes may be found solid happiness and sturdy sincerity rarely experienced in warmer climes or among a more enthusiastic people.

THE ROYAL EXCHANGE, LONDON.–The fine building here represented was built in 1842, and is preceded by a fine Corinthian portico, approached by a broad flight of steps. On the architrave is the inscription, "The earth is the Lord's and the fullness thereof." In London some of the tenants of the hereditary landed system say that this inscription means the landlords. The interior of the Exchange forms a quadrangular-covered court surrounded by colonnades; in the center is a fine marble statue of Queen Victoria, and in the corners are statues of Queen Elizabeth and Charles II. The building was opened by Queen Elizabeth in 1571. At the oppostite end of the Exchange from that here pictured is "Lloyd's Shipping Exchange", the central point of every kind of business connected with navigation, maritime trade, marine insurance and shipping intelligence, and immediately back of that in an open space is a statue to the memory of the American philanthropist, George Peabody, which was erected by public subscription. He gave at different times upward of two and a half million dollars for the erection of suitable dwellings for the working classes in the metropolis. The space in front of the Exchange is one of the chief points of convergence of the London omnibus traffic, which during business hours is so large that at times blockades take place which make it impossible to pass this point in a carriage or omnibus for from 15 to 30 minutes.

TRAFALGAR SQUARE, LONDON.—This is one of the finest open spaces in the City of London, and, therefore, a center of great attraction. It commemorates, so to speak, the battle of Trafalgar, gained by the English over the combined armies of France and Spain, by which victory Napoleon's purpose of invading England was frustrated. From the terrace, on the north side of the Square, rises the National Gallery, which, among the buildings around the Square, is the principal point of size in architectural merit. The building is in the Corinthian style, four hundred and sixty feet in length. The nucleus of the gallery which it contains was formed by the purchase of thirty-eight pictures in 1824, since which time it has been rapidly extended by donations, legacies and purchases, and is now composed of about fifteen hundred pictures, among which are some of the art gems of the world. Among the important collections here preserved is that of J.W. Turner, who bequeathed his remaining works to the gallery.

CATHEDRAL OF NOTRE DAME, PARIS.—This cathedral, founded in 1163 on the site of a church of the fourth century, was consecrated in 1182, but the building was not completed until the thirteenth century, and has since been frequently altered and completely restored in 1845. It can scarcely be said that the general effect is commensurate with the reputation of the edifice. This is owing partly to structural defects, partly to the lowness of its situation and partly to the absence of spires; it is, moreover, now surrouded by lofty buildings, which further dwarf its dimensions, and lastly the surrounding soil has gradually been raised to the level of the pavement of the interior, whereas when built the church

was approached by a flight of thirteen steps. During the French revolution this cathedral was sadly desecrated. A decree was passed in August, 1793, consigning the venerable pile to destruction, but this was afterward rescinded, and the sculptures only were demolished. On the 10th of November, the same year, the church was converted into a Temple of Reason, and the statue of the Virgin replaced by one of Liberty, while the patriotic songs of the National Guards were sung instead of the usual sacred music. On a mound thrown up in the choir burned the "Torch of Truth", over which rose "Temple of Philosophy", adorned with busts of Voltaire, Rousseau and others.

43

THE CHAMPS-ELYSEES, PARIS.—This magnificent avenue, which is flanked with handsome buildings, is one of the most fashionable promenades in Paris, especially between three and seven o'clock, when numerous carriages, riders and pedestrians are on their way to the Bois de Boulogne, which begins just beyond the Arch of Triumph shown at the end of the avenue in this picture. The lower end of the Champs-Elysees abounds with the attractions of cafés, jugglers, shows, restaurants, etc. These various entertainments are most popular toward evening, by gaslight, and are in great request until nearly midnight. Travelers always have here an opportunity of witnessing one of the characteristic phases of Parisian life.

To the right, separated from the Champs-Elysees by a large garden, is the Palace of the Elysees, erected in 1708, and now occupied as the official residence of the President of the Republic. During the reign of Louis XV this mansion was the residence of Madame de Pompadour, from whose heirs it was purchased by the king to form a residence for the foreign ambassadors. Under Louis XVI the palace acquired the name of Elizabeth Bourbon from its prolonged occupancy by the Duchess de Bourbon. The palace was afterward occupied in turn by Murat, Napoleon I, Louis Bonaparte, King of Holland and his Queen, Hortense, Alexander I of Russia and the Duc de Berry.

44

THE HOTEL DE VILLE, OR, CITY HALL, PARIS.—This building is in many respects one of the finest in Paris, and was erected on the site of the old one, which was burned by the Communists in 1871. It may be described as an enlarged reproduction of the old building with richer ornamentations and more convenient arrangement. The front, in the center of which is a handsome clock, is adorned with rich sculptures; in the niches of the principal stories are statues of celebrated Parisians of all ages. The roof is surmounted by ten gilded figures of Heralds. The Hotel de Ville has played a conspicuous part in different French revolutions. On July 14, 1789, the captors of the Bastille were conducted in triumph into its great hall; three days later King Louis XVI came in possession from Versailles to the Hotel de Ville, under the protection of popular deputies, thus publicly testifying his submission to the will of the national assembly. The king was accompanied by a dense mob, to whom he showed himself in the window of the Hotel de Ville wearing the tri-colored cockade, which LaFayette had just chosen as cognizance of the new national guard. Here was also celebrated the union of the July monarchy. Louis Phillippe presented himself at one of the windows of the Hotel de Ville in August, 1830, and in view of the populace embraced LaFayette.

THE GRAND OPERA HOUSE, PARIS.—The here-pictured sumptuous edifice was begun in 1861 and occupied thirteen years in its construction. It is now the largest theatre in the world, but contains seats for only twenty-two hundred people, being less than the number accommodated by the opera house at Vienna, or the vast theatres of La Scala, Milan, and San Carlo, at Naples. Nothing can surpass the magnificence of the materials with which the building is elaborately decorated, and for which the whole of Europe was laid under contribution. Sweden and Scotland yielded a supply of green and red granite; from Italy was brought the yellow and white marble, from Finland red porphyry, from Spain brocatello, and from different parts of France other marbles of various colors. in 1860 competitive plans for the new opera were sent in by the most eminent architects in France, and it was resolved that the edifice should in every respect be the most magnificent of the kind in the world. The magnificent interior is exceedingly effective, and it altogether an unrivaled work of its kind. The cost of the site now occupied by the building was two million, one hundred thousand dollars, and the cost of construction seven million, three hundred thousand dollars. The staff of performers is about twenty-five hundred in number. The government allows an annual subisdy of one hundred and sixty thousand dollars toward the support of the opera.

46

THE PLACE DE LA BASTILE, PARIS.–The here pictured square in Paris was formerly the site of the Bastile, a stronghold which was erected in 1371 and used as a state prison for the confinement of the persons of rank who had fallen victims of the intrigues of the court or caprices of the government, and attained a world-wide celebrity in consequence of its destruction in July, 1789, at the beginning of the French revolution. The July column, the rising in the center of the square, is so called in commemoration of the month in which the Bastile was overthrown. It rises to a height of one hundred and fifty-four feet and rests on massive round substruction of white marble. The vaults underneath the column contain a sarcophagus forty-five feet in length and seven feet in width. In this receptacle were placed the remains of the victims of the revolution of 1848. In May, 1871, during the Communists' reign of terror, these vaults were filled with gunpowder and combustibles by the insurgents for the purpose of blowing up the column and converting the whole neighborhood into a heap of ruins. Fortunately the attempt was unsuccessful.

47

PLACE DE LA CONCORDE, PARIS.—The here pictured Place is the most beautiful and extensive in Paris, and one of the finest in the world. It covers an area of three hundred and ninety yards in width. Numerous historical associations, mostly of a sombre character, are connected with this Place. On the 21st of January, 1793, the guillotine began its bloody work here with the execution of Louis XVI. On July 17th Charlotte Corday was beheaded. On the 16th of October the ill-fated queen, Marie Antoinette; on the 14th of November, Phillip, Duke of Orleans, father of King Louis Phillip, and on the 12th of May Madame Elizabeth, sister of Louis XVI. Between January 21, 1793, and May 3, 1795, upward of twenty-eight hundred persons perished here by the guillotine. The obelisk shown in the foreground is a monolith, or single block of red granite from the quarries of Assuan in upper Egypt. It is seventy-six feet in height and weight two hundred and forty tons. A vessel was occupied nearly two years in bringing this, the pasha's gift, to France from Egypt, and it was five years from the time the vessel started until its erection on its present site was accomplished, the expense of the whole undertaking amounting to upward of four hundred thousand dollars. The fountains form another striking ornament of the Place. Each of them consists of a basin fifty-three feet in diameter.

48

THE STOCK EXCHANGE OR BOURSE, PARIS.—The handsome building here pictured in Graeco-Roman style, is surrounded by a series of sixty-six Corinthian columns and was built in imitation of the Temple of Vespasian in the Forum at Rome. It was begun in 1808 and occupied eighteen years in construction. Its length is two hundred and twenty-five feet, width one hundred and thirty-five feet, and height one hundred feet. The columns are each thirty-three feet in height and three and one-third feet in thickness. The edifice is enclosed by an iron railing and approached by a flight of sixteen steps at each end. At the corners in front are allegorical statues of Commerce and Consular Justice. The hall of the Exchange, which is one hundred and five feet in length and fifty-seven feet wide, is open for business daily at twelve o'clock except on Sundays and holidays. A few minutes before that hour the open space here shown in front of the Bourse begins to present a busy scene. Numerous vehicles, chiefly private carriages, drive up and the money-seeking throng hasten into the building. Business, however, does not fairly begin until about half past twelve. The parquet at the end of the hall is a railed-off space which the brokers alone are privileged to enter. The annual amount of business here transacted is calculated at ten billion dollars. The space in front of the Bourse is a great center for the Parisian omnibus lines.

49

PALACE AND GALLERIES OF THE LOUVRE, PARIS.—The Louvre, the most important public building in Paris, both architecturally and on account of its treasures of art, is a palace of vast extent, bordering on the Seine, and derives its name from the ancient hunting chateau once situated here in the midst of a forest then infested by wolves. On the same site, close to the city wall, at that period Phillip Augustus erected a castle, consisting of four wings, enclosing a quadrangular court. The castle was afterward handsomely fitted up as a royal residence by Charles V, but was removed in 1541, and the foundation of the present palace laid by Francis I, who intended the court of the new building to be of the same extent as that of the old. The Louvre now covers an area of about forty-eight acres, enclosing different courts, and forming one of the most magnificent palaces in the world. In the square in the foregorund of this picture is a monument to Gambetta. Since 1793 the apartments of the old Louvre have been used as a museum and the offices of the ministers of finance. On the 24th of May, 1871, the whole building, with its immense treasures of art, was seriously imperiled by the incendiarisms of the Communists. The part of the connecting wing next to the Tuilleries was much damaged by the fire, and the imperial library, which the palace contained, together with the precious manuscripts, was destroyed.

THE PALACE OF VERSAILLES, FRANCE.—The site of Versailles was hardly favorable for a palace, and still less so for the magnificent park which surrounds the palace. The palace and park cost the treasury of King Louis XIV the enormous sum of two hundred million dollars, and its annual maintenance also involved heavy expenditures. No less than thirty-six thousand men and six thousand horses were employed at one time in forming the terraces of the garden, leveling the park and constructing a road to it from Paris and the aqueduct from Maintenon, a distance of thirty-one miles from Versailles. This aqueduct was intended to bring the water of the River Eure to Versailles, but was discontinued owing to the great mortality among the soldiers employed. The Palace of Versailles presents an imposing appearance when seen from the garden, the standpoint from which this photograph is taken, the front of the palace being a quarter of a mile in length. The building dates from several periods, and its style lacks uniformity. This palace is intimately associated with the history of France. It witnessed the zenith and decadence of the reign of Louis XIV, and under his successor the magnificent "palace of the grand monarch" became the scene of the disreputable Pompadour and De Barry dominations.

THE BOURSE, OR EXCHANGE, BERLIN.—On the bank of the River Spree rises this imposing Berlin Bourse. Erected in 1860, it was the first modern building of Berlin erected in stone instead of brick. The chief side, here photographed, is embellished with a double colonnade, above which in the center is a group in sandstone representing Borussia as the protectoress of agriculture and commerce. The interior of the building is especially interesting. Entering it one passes through the ante-chamber to the great hall, which is the largest in Berlin, and is three hundred and thirty feet in length and eighty-eight feet in width, lined with imitation marble, and divided by arcades into three parts adorned with fine frescoes. More than

4,000 brokers congregate here daily. During the business hours, from twelve to two o'clock, the floor presents an animated scene. The corn and provision dealers' exchanges are in the center of the building on the other side of the street. The building contains the largest hall in Berlin, the gallery above which is often filled with spectators who come there to watch the trade of the brokers below. The bridge in the foreground of the building is one of fifty that cross the River Spree that divides Berlin into two parts. It is a stream with scarcely any current, and is navigable for steamboats for about one hundred miles from its mouth.

THE CITY OF BERLIN.—Berlin, the capital of Prussia and residence of the Emperor of Germany, is the seat of the imperial government as well as the highest Prussian authorities. It occupies the third place among the chief cities of Europe; its situation is very favorable and one of the chief causes of the town's prosperity. It is an important center of the railway system of Germany and one of the foremost seats of commerce in the country, and, unquestionably, the greatest manufacturing town on the continent of Europe. The money market of Berlin is of the utmost importance, and the traffic on the River Spree and its canals is even busier than on the far-famed Rhine. The boundaries of the city now enclose an area of about twenty-five square miles, the buildings having filled up the whole of the Spree valley, which here averages three miles in breadth, and the valley is here intersected by various water courses which are beginning to encroach on the surrounding plains raised some thirty to forty feet higher. In external appearance Berlin is by no means deficient in interest. In situation, though not especially picturesque, it has the charm of mediaeval and historical associations. There is no end of architectural display, and the last fifteen years have witnessed the erection of handsome buildings in every part of the city; those erected by private enterprises often presenting considerable individual style and taste. It may be a great surprise to Americans to know that this German city has grown at nearly as great a rate as our American phenomenon Chicago.

53

THE NATIONAL GALLERY, BERLIN.—In the center of a beautiful square, surrounded with Doric colonnades and embellished with statues, flower beds and a fountain, rises the well-known Berlin National Gallery, which was designed by the famous German architect, Stuler, in accordance with a plan of Frederick William IV. The building is in the form of a Corinthian dome, two hundred feet long, one hundred and five feet wide, elevated on a basement thirty-nine feet in height. At the south end is a portico of eight columns, and at the north a semi-circular apse. At the head of the imposing flight of steps in front is the equestrian stuatue of Frederick William IV, erected in 1886. The rich and appropriate decorations of the interior are executed in more solid material than those of the ordinary museum. The collection in the gallery, the nucleus of which was formed by two hundred and fifty pictures bequeathed by a man named Wagener to the Emperor William I, then Prince Regent, now consists of over five hundred paintings and many drawings and sculptures. The collection is constantly increasing, and it is a pleasure to relate that the pictures are frequently loaned to exhibitions of collections of paintings outside of Berlin, thus enabling those who are not fortunate enough to be able to visit the German metropolis an opportunity of studying some of the nation's art treasures.

PALACE OF PRINCE BISMARCK, BERLIN.—The palace of the Emperor of Gemany is, of course, an object of great interest in Berlin, but scarcely overshadows in point of interest this unpretentious home of Prince Bismarck, the ex-chancellor of the German empire and foremost of German statesmen. Bismarck received his education at various German universities, and after finishing his studies lived for a time on his estates. Before 1847 he was little heard of, but about that time began to attract attention in the Prussian Parliament as an ultra-royalist. During the Franco-German war of 1870–71 he was the spokesman of Germany, and he it was who dictated the terms of peace with France. Having been made a count in 1866, Bismarck was later on created prince and chancellor of the German empire. After the peace of Frankfort in May, 1871, the bent of his policy, domestic and foreign, was to consolidate the young empire of his own creating by rendering its institutions more beneficent, authoritative, homogeneous and stable, and to secure it through alliance and political combinations against attack from without. The resignation of Bismarck of his office as prime minister was announced in February, 1890, but did not actually occur until March 17th, when divergence of opinion between him and the emperor led to his retirement. His departure from Berlin on the 29th was made the occasion of a great popular demonstration in his favor.

55

ROYAL LIBRARY IN BERLIN.—This fine building is situated in the Opera Place, adjoining the palace of Emperor William I. It was erected in 1780, in imitation of the royal winter riding school at Vienna, and is among the finest rococo structures in Berlin, though somewhat likened to a chest of drawers. The motto below the tympanum, "Nietrumentum Spiritus", was selected by Frederick the Great. The library which was founded in 1651, contains over a million volumes and nearly twenty thousand manuscripts, among which may be mentioned the manuscript and first impression of Luther's translation of the Bible, Guttenberg's Bible on parchment, dated 1450, the first book which was ever printed with movable type, and a manuscript of the Gospel of the eighth century, said to have been presented by Charlemagne to the Saxon duke, Wittenkind, and many important musical works. Some of the older pieces of music are of great historical interest. The last statistics relating to literature published in Berlin state that of two thousand books published in the city twenty per cent. refer to literature, fifteen per cent. to philology, seven per cent. to history and four per cent. to medicine. Turning to journals and periodical literature, nearly three hundred newspapers and magazines, daily, weekly or monthly, appear annually.

56

ROYAL MUSEUM IN BERLIN.—The exterior of this edifice is not particularly significant, and its chief attraction consists in the rich and artistic interior decorations. These are elaborate to a scale of grandeur, and their tendency is to throw the articles exhibited in the museum into the shade. One of the principal points of interest in this building is the cabinet of engravings, which is open to the public on Sundays, and on other days to students only. The collection, which is one of the most extensive in Europe, embraces engravings and wood-cuts by masters from the fifteenth century to date, drawings by artists who died before 1800, many paintings from the tenth to the sixteenth century, and early illustrated books. In 1877 an important collection of engravings and wood-cuts of Albert Durer was purchased, accompanied by forty of his engravings. In 1882 the German government bought the celebrated manuscript collection of the Duke of Hamilton, containing nearly seven hundred manuscripts. Those of purely scientific or literary value were deposited in the Royal Library, and those interesting from their artistic merit were placed in the cabinet of engravings in this museum. The gem of the collection is a unique copy of Dante, with eighty-four illustrations by Botticelli, of Florence.

ROYAL PALACE, BERLIN.—This grand establishment is in the form of a rectangle six hundred and eighty feet in length and three hundred and eighty feet in depth. It rises four stories to a height of one hundred feet, while the dome above it is two hundred and thirty feet in height. The original building on this site was a castle erected in 1451. Frederick I, King of Prussia, determined to replace that irregular pile of buildings by a uniform structure of massive and imposing portals, and began the work in 1699. The work of alteration, thus projected, has, however, never been fully carried out. In the time of Frederick the Great the palace served as a residence for almost all the members of the royal family, containing all the royal collections, and it was also the seat of several government officials. The Emperor William II, who ascended the throne in June, 1888, has also made this palace his imperial residence, occupuying the rooms on the first floor overlooking the garden. The exterior of the palace is in general effect massive and most imposing. In addition to its schools and universities, Berlin is rich in institutions for the promotion of learning, science and the arts. It possesses numerous public museums and galleries and, next to Leipsic, is the largest book publishing center in Germany. It is not only a center of intelligence, but also an important center of manufacturing trade.

UNTER-DEN-LINDEN, BERLIN.—This handsome and spacious part of Berlin, which likewise comprises the most interesting historical association, is the long line of street extending from the Brandenburg gate to the Royal Palace (which it fronts), is the famous "Unter-den-Liden". The "Linden" is a street one hundred and ninety-six feet in width, which derives its name from the avenue of lime trees with which it is planted, and resembles more than any other street in Berlin the crowded Parisian boulevards. It is flanked with handsome palaces, spacious hotels and attractive stores, between which the long vista of a number of side streets are visible at intervals. The gross length of the street is about two-thirds of a mile and presents an animated picture in the evening when brilliantly lighted by electricity. The Brandenburg gate at the west end of the Linden forms the entrance to the town from the Thier Garten. It was erected in 1789 in imitation of the propylaea at Athens, and has five passages, that in the center being reserved for royal carriages. At the end of the Linden rises the statue of Frederick the Great, forty-four feet in height, cast of bronze. It is an impressive and masterly work by Rouch, and probably the greatest monument of its kind in Europe. The king is represented on horseback, with his coronation robes and a walking stick.

59

ROYAL PALACE AT CHARLOTTENBURG, NEAR BERLIN.—This well-known palace consists of a large group of buildings of a total length of five hundred and fifty yards. The here photographed central portion was erected in 1699 and was enlarged in 1706 and at that time provided with its effective dome. The building contains a theatre which was added in 1788. The Emperor Frederick III (beloved of all Germans) spent the last ten weeks of his illness here. The decorations of the interior of the old central portion and in the apartments once occupied by Frederick the Great, are grand beyond description. They are fitted up in the style of Louis XVI. The mausoleum where Queen Louise and her husband Frederick William III repose, is near this palace. The recumbent figures of this illustrious pair, executed in marble, are strikingly impressive. The beautiful figure of the queen executed by Roche's master hand at Carrara and Rome in 1812 was placed here in 1815, and at once established the sculptor's fame. The heart of Frederick William IV is placed in an urn at the foot of the marble in this mausoleum.

COLOGNE, GERMANY.—This city, which is famous for its cathedral, is the largest town in the Rhenish province of Prussia and one of the most important commercial places in Germany. It lies on the bank of the Rhine, across which a bridge of boats and an iron bridge lead to suburbs on the opposite bank. From a distance, and especially when approached by steamboats, the town with its numerous towers presents an exceedingly pleasing appearance. Many of the old streets contain interesting speciments of architecture dating from as remote times as the thirteenth century. The development of the town received a great impetus in 1881, when the adoption of a new and very advanced line of fortifications literally doubled the area of the town. The cathedral, which justly excites the admiration of every beholder, is the most magnificent Gothic edifice in the world. It stands on an eminence about sixty feet above the Rhine, which is partly composed of Roman remains. The entire sum expended in its construction was $4,500,000. The largest of the bells in the tower was cast with the metal of captured French guns and weighs twenty-five tons. It requires twenty-eight people to set it in motion. The towers are five hundred and twelve feet in height and are the loftiest church towers in Europe.

BRUHL TERRACE, DRESDEN.—Dresden, the capital of the Kingdom of Saxony, has rapidly increased in importance during the present century. The city lies on both banks of the River Elbe, which about equally divides it. Its beautiful environs and magnificent picture galleries attract thousands of visitors annually, and a very considerable English-speaking community reside here permanently. Bruhl Terrace, which is here pictured, was originally laid out as a garden in 1738 by Count Bruhl, the minister of Augustine III. It rises above the Elbe, and, fully half a mile in length, is a favorite promenade, and commands a fine view of the river.

It is approached by a broad flight of steps, adorned with gilded groups of Night, Morning, Noon and Evening in sandstone, by Schilling. The terrace is planted with trees, and on the side next the town is the Bruhl Palace and the Academy of Art. In the history of architecture Dresden has attained a high reputation from having been the headquarters of the famous architect, Semper, who was one of the greatest German architects of the present century. About the beginning of the present century, Dresden began to regain is former reputation in the province of art, of which, at one time, it was the acknowledged headquarters.

MUSEUM IN DRESDEN.—This handsome edifice in the renaissance style was designed by Semper, begun in 1847, and completed in 1854. It is considered one of the finest examples of modern architecture. On a sub-structure of blocks of freestone rises the vast oblong building, which consists of two principal stories and a third of smaller dimensions, with a lofty carriage approach in the center and surmounted by a cupola. The museum forms the northeast wing of the Zwinger, a building, or rather a collection of buildings, erected by Augustus II, but it was left unfinished for more than a century. It consists of seven pavilions, connected by a gallery of one story, and, according to the still existing plans of the master, the present site of the museum was to have been occupied by a huge portal, which was to lead to an elevated plateau flanked by two long palaces. These edifices were to have been connected by galleries, whence flights of steps would have descended to the River Elbe. The great masters of the golden period of Italian art are in the Dresden picture gallery admirably represented. The museum and the Zwinger contain the gems of the Dresden collections. In the museum, picture gallery, Zwinger, etc., are various other collections of interest which do not properly come under the head of art.

FRANKFORT-ON-THE-MAIN.—This well-known town, which down to 1866 was one of the free towns of the German Federation, now belongs to Prussia. The city lies in a spacious plain bounded by mountains. From a commerical, and particularly a financial point of view, Frankfort is one of the most important cities in Germany. The Rothschilds formerly lived and still conduct a banking business at Frankfort. The older part of the town consists of narrow streets which are quite unattractive, but the new streets of the city have many handsome modern buildings. The town is artistically laid out, with beautiful public gardens. An air of wealth and importance pervades the city, and affords illustration of the success of its commercial relations. Notwithstanding its large Jewish population, in the market place in front of the palace, down to the end of the last century no Jew was permitted to enter. It was the scene of those great public rejoicings in the election of the emperor, which Goethe so beautifully describes in his autobiography. The city was also the the site of an imperial palace, which was built by Charlemagne and renewed by Louis the Pious in 822. The palace was mortgaged by the emperors of the fourteenth century, and so frequently altered that no external trace of the original edifice now remains.

THE HAMBURG WAREHOUSES.—This harbor, where numerous vessels from all quarters of the globe lie, presents a busy and picturesque scene. The docks, recently extended, now stretch along the bank of the River Elbe for a distance of over five miles, and accommodate upward of four hundred sea-going vessels as well as a large number of barges and other river craft. Hamburg is one of the world's famous ports and the one from which cholera was brought to the United States in 1892. The new harbor for sailing vessels has room for six hundred ships. The area includes large warehouses, some of which are here pictured, dry-docks, ship-building yards, etc. and the whole is lighted at night by electricity. Down to the beginning of the present century Hamburg enjoyed considerable reputation in the literary world. In 1678 the first theatre in Germany for opera was founded here. The history of the city, together with the enterprising character of its inhabitants, sufficiently account for the almost entire disappearance of all relics previous to that date, and for its thoroughly modern aspect. After the Peace of Vienna, Hamburg rapidly increased in extent, and notwithstanding the appalling fire by which the city was devastated in 1842, and other disasters, she has never ceased to prosper since she gained her independence.

JUNGFENSTRASSE, HAMBURG.—The city of Hamburg has over half a million inhabitants, and next to London, Liverpool and Glasgow, is the most important commercial place in Europe. The street here pictured is that which borders the harbor; the city being advantageously situated on the River Elbe, in which the tide rises twice daily so as to admit of the entrance of vessels of considerable tonnage. The city is connected by railways with every port of Europe. Besides the Elbe, there are two small rivers at Hamburg, called the Ulster and Binne; the former forms a large basin outside the town and a smaller one within it. Nothing certain is known of the origin of Hamburg, but as early as 1118 Charlemagne founded a castle here. The city was honorably distinguished in the good work of sweeping the sea of pirates. The discovery of America and of the sea-route to India was not without its beneficial effect in stimulating the trade of Hamburg, which, however, does not compete with that of England and Holland. Dissensions frequently arose between the council and the citizens in the middle ages, which proved very detrimental to the welfare of the city; but towards the middle of the last century its prosperity began to return. The surface of the water is enlivened with steel launches, row boats and groups of swans. The docks are a favorite promenade, especially on fine summer evenings, when they present a picturesque appearance.

HEIDLEBERG.–Few towns can vie with Heidelberg in the beauty of its environs and historical interest. Count Otho transferred the seat of his government to Heidelberg in 1228; it thus became the capital of the palatine and so continued for nearly five centuries. Heidelberg forms the key of the mountainous valley of the Necker river, which, below the town, opens into the plains of the famous Rhine. The castled hill leaves little space between its base and the river for the further extension of the town, excepting along the river's bank. The famous University of Heidelberg is the cradle of science in southern Germany. It is, after the universities of Prague and Leipsic, the oldest in Germany, and was founded in 1386. Its library has over three hundred thousand volumes and three thousand manuscrips, also fifteen hundred ancient documents; a large number of the manuscripts it formerly contained were transferred to Rome as a present from Maximilian to the Pope after the capture of Heidelberg, scarcely a third of which have since been returned. During the stormy times of the Thirty Years War the town survived with difficulty. In the summer of 1886, the university's 500th anniversay was celebrated with great ceremony.

67

AUGUSTUS PLACE, LEIPSIC.—This spacious open space in Leipsic is surrounded by the magnificent new theatre, the museum, the post-office and several fine private residences. The new theatre is a handsome building, completed in 1867, the principal front being adorned with a Corinthian portico. The chief attraction of the museum, the building opposite the theatre, is its collection of fine pictures. This gallery was established in 1837, and since then has been constantly increased by purchase and by the presentation of a collection of French pictures. The Augusteum, which faces on this place, is the seat of the University of Leipsic, which was founded in 1408 and is now attended by over three thousand students. Its library contains about four hundred thousand volumes and four thousand manuscripts. Leipsic was the scene of a battle in 1813, which was one of the most prolonged and sanguinary on record. It was conducted on both sides by some of the greatest generals of modern times, and Napoleon had a force of about one hundred and fifty thousand men. The Russians, Austrians and Prussians who were opposed to Napoleon had over three hundred thousand troops. Napoleon lost about sixty thousand soldiers. On the 19th of October, 1813, a Prussian landguard battalion forced an entrance into the town, and at twelve o'clock Napoleon retreated. The bridge, the only mode of crossing the river, was blown up, in consequence of which thousands of the French perished by drowning, and twenty-five thousand who had not yet crossed the bridge were taken prisoners.

ITY OF MUNICH, GERMANY.—Munich, the capital of Bavaria, has a population approaching four hundred thousand and lies on the River Iser on the south side of a sterile plain, which is some fifty square miles in area. The lofty situation of the city and its close proximity to the Alps render it liable to sudden changes of temperature. Munich was founded by "Henry the Lion", who constructed a bridge over the river at this point and established a custom-house, a mint, and a salt depot on the site of the city in 1158. The land is said to have belonged to the monks of Schaftlarn, whence came the names of "Forum Monacos", or Munich. Under the Wittenbach princes the town prospered. Otho the Illustrious,

who died in 1253, transferred his residence to Munich, and his son, Lewis the Severe, built the old palace which is to-day the oldest existing palace of the dukes of Bavaria and is now occupied by public offices. After a fire in 1327, Emperor Lewis, the Bavarian, almost entirely re-erected the city, which was loyally and devotedly attached to him; but for its modern magnificence Munich is chiefly indebted to Ludwig I, who died in 1868, that monarch who even before his accession had purchased many valuable works of art and attracted many artists to Munich, and raised the city during twenty-four years to the foremost rank as a school of German art.

MARKET PLACE, NUREMBERG.—The first authentic mention of Nuremberg, which seems to have been called into existence by the foundation of its castle, occurs in a document of 1050, and about the same period it received from Henry III permission to establish a custom house and a market place, the one here photographed. Formerly among the richest and most influential of the free imperial towns, Nuremberg is one of the few cities of Europe that have retained their mediaeval aspect substantially unimpaired. It is still surrounded with ancient feudal walls and a moat, though of late several bridges have had to be made to meet the exigencies of modern traffic. Three hundred and sixty-five towers formerly strengthened the walls, of which nearly one hundred are still in place, and a few of the interesting old gateways have also been preserved. Many of the streets are narrow and crowded and the majority of the houses have their gables turned toward the street. A praiseworthy desire to maintain the quaint picturesqueness of the town has induced most of the builders of new houses to imitate the lofty peaked gables and red tile roofs of the older dwellings, and it is easy for a visitor to Nuremberg to fancy himself carried back to the middle ages.

BABLESBURG PALACE AT POTSDAM.—This picturesque chateau was erected in the English Gothic style in 1835 and greatly extended in 1848. It stands in the middle of a beautiful park laid out by the famous landscape gardener Buckler. The interior of the castle is simply but most tastefully decorated, and contains many fine works of art, most of which are those of the Berlin and Dusseldorf schools. Emperor William I invariably spent the latter half of the summer here, and his study and bedroom are still shown to visitors. Memorials of the campaigns of 1864–66–70–71 are also shown to visitors. Charming views through the dense forliage surrounding this palace, of Potsdam, Sans Souci, the well-known Marble Palace, and the broad expanse of the River Havel with its wooded hills, are to be had. The water in the fountain in front of the palace is forced to a height of one hundred feet from the Havel, by means of a steam engine. Potsdam is the seat of government for the Prussian province of Brandenberg and the summer residence of the Emperor of Germany. It lies sixteen miles to the southwest of Berlin. The town is handsomely built, though with a monotonous regularity that betrays its artificial origin. During the summer months its streets are enlivened by endless streams of excursionists from Berlin. Potsdam is a city of beautiful palaces.

PALACE OF SANS SOUCI, POTSDAM.—The literal translation of the words "Sans Souci" is "without care", and unquestionably it is with an idea to accomplish the end signified by that translation that the construction of this palace was begun by King Frederick the Great, by whom it was erected in 1745, and was thereafter that monarch's almost constant residence. It stands on a commanding eminence above the town of Potsdam. Though it is still a place of great beauty, the main interest of the palace consists in the numerous reminiscences which it contains of its illustrious founder, who died here. A clock which he was in the habit of winding up is said to have stopped at the precise moment of his death, which occurred at 2:30 P.M., August 7, 1736. The palace contains a portrait of him painted in his fifty-sixth year, which is said to be the only one for which he ever sat. The walls are hung with pictures by famous artists, Watteau among others, and the library contains a few ancient busts. In the dining-room stands a bronze bust of Charles XII of Sweden, who was a great friend of Frederick the Great. The west end contains the room in which Frederick William IV died, and which has not been changed since his death; it is also the same room that was occupied by Voltaire on a visit to the King of Prussia. The picture gallery has yielded up its finest work to the museum at Berlin.

THE CATHEDRAL IN STRASBURG.—By far the most prominent building in this old German city is the here pictured cathedral, which in its present form represents the activity of four centuries, part of the building dating from 1015; the tower having been added in 1435. The nave is a fine specimen of pure Gothic architecture. The apse shows the transition from the Romanesque to the Gothic style. The upper part of the facade and the tower were completed in accordance with a different plan. The sculptural ornamentaions both within and without are very rich. The early history of Strasburg, as is the case with most Episcopal cities, consists mainly of a record of the struggle between the bishops and the citizens the latter as they grew in wealth and power feeling the fetters of ecclesiastical rule inconsistent with their full development. It was at Strasburg, that Louis Napoleon made his first ineffectual attempt to grasp power. In the war of 1870, Strasburg, with its garrison of seventeen thousand men, surrendered to the Germans after a siege of seven weeks. The town and cathedral suffered considerably from the bombardment, but all traces of the havoc have been removed.

STUTTGART, GERMANY.—This populous German city is the capital of Wurtemberg, and has nearly one hundred and fifty thousand inhabitants, mainly Protestants. It is a city of comparitively modern origin, beautifully situated and surrounded by picturesque vineclad and wooden hedges. Its name first occurs in a charter dated 1229, and from 1265 to 1325 it was the favorite residence of the counts of Wurtemberg, and became the capital of the country in 1482, and at length in the reign of King Frederick, attained its present form. In the revival of renaissance forms of art, Stuttgart has taken a prominent part from its numerous talented artists. The name and idea of the German renaissance has only of late years become familiar in Germany itself, and consequently not known at all beyond its bounds. Formerly German critics were staisfied with the French or German style, and drew no sharp line of demarkation between these later works and the products of the middle ages proper. Particular parts of buildings, such as the portal and bay-windows, were strongly manifested in order to display the knowledge of the fashionable Italian art. It was not until about the beginning of the seventeenth century, when German architects had begun to prosecute their study in Italy, that the Italian renaissance style became at all familiar in Germany, and copied columns, friezes and moldings used by Italian architects.

THEATRE, GUATEMALA.–The theatre in Guatemala is a modern building, in imitation of the Church of La Madeleine, Paris. Like most buildings in Central America it is built of Mamposteria, a mixture of brick, mortar and stone covered with stucco. The building stands in the center of a plaza which is planted with shrubs and flowering plants and has a fountain. The palcos, or boxes, are on the second tier or what would be known here as the first gallery; back of this runs a corridor used as a promenade between the acts, and is arranged with accommodations for serving refreshments if desired. Above are two other galleries also provided with stalls or boxes. The pit is used exclusively by men and is provided with comfortable chairs, such as appear here in some of the theatres. The building is handsomely decorated and artistically draped. As an encouragement to dramatic art, the government subsidizes the building in about from twenty-five thousand to forty thousand dollars per year for the engagement of first-class artists for from five to six months annually.

VIEW OF AMSTERDAM, HOLLAND.—Amsterdam, the commercial capital of Holland, lies at the influx of the Amtel into the Ij river, which is an arm of the Zuider Zee and forms an excellent harbor. The town originated at the beginning of the thirteenth century, when the Lord of Amstel built a castle there and constructed the dam which has given rise to its name. In 1311 it was united with Holland. In the fourteenth century the town began to assume great importance and was sought as an asylum by exiled marshals of Brabant. In 1421 the place suffered a serious conflagration, but its prosperity soon returned, and at the beginning of the Spanish troubles Amsterdam had become a most important city. As the chief mart for the colonial products of the Dutch colonies, such as tobaccos, Java coffee, sugar, rice, spices, etc., Amsterdam is even to-day one of the first commercial places in Europe. Its industries are also considerable, including refineries of sugar and camphor, tobacco manufactories, and for what it is perhaps the most famous, diamond polishing mills. The houses are all constructed on foundations of piles, a fact which gave rise to the jest of Arasmus that he knew a city whose inhabitants dwelt on the tops of trees like rooks. The upper stratum of the natural soil is loam and loose sand, upon which no permanent building can be erected unless a solid sub-structure be first formed by driving piles.

THE CITY HALL, DELFT, HOLLAND.–Delft, a town in Holland, situated nearly ten miles from Rotterdam and on the line of the canal between that city and The Hague, is a well and regularly built town in the form of a square, but has a rather peculiar appearance from its streets being traversed by the narrow stagnant canals so common in Holland. The city's public buildings comprise the palace where William of Orange was assassinated, the city hall here shown, which was erected in 1618, and the old church dating from the eleventh century, which is directly opposite the city hall. The church is especially interesting for its chime of five hundred bells and as being the burial place of the princes of the House of Orange, from the days of the Liberator down to the present century. For a long time the name of Delft was associated, not only in Holland but almost universally, with the manufacture of excellent earthenware, the blue Delft china being a well-known feature of our grandmother's closet; but this industry, as well as others which were of great importance during the last century, has become almost extinct. The town was almost totally destroyed by fire in 1536. A melancholy interest is attached to the palace which was the scene of the death of William the Silent (the founder of Dutch independence), who was assassinated in it in 1584. The palace was long used as a barrack, but is now being restored.

VIEW OF ROTTERDAM, HOLLAND.—Rotterdam is, after Amsterdam, the most important commercial place in Europe. It is situated about fourteen miles from the North sea. The city is, as are most other Holland cities, intersected by numerous canals, all deep enough for the passage of heavily laden barges. Communication between the different quarters of the town is maintained by draw or swing bridges. The average number of vessels which enter the port annually is six thousand. The most important cargoes are coffee, sugar, tobacco, rice and spices. In most of the Dutch cities the roads and streets skirting the canals are planted with trees, which render them shady and picturesque. The houses are generally narrow and lofty, constructed of red brick and white cement. The windows of the ground floors are generally of airy dimensions, and polished with that scrupulous care which characterizes the Dutch of all classes, the houses always presenting a very cheerful and prosperous appearance. At the cellar doors in the side of the street, sideboards with the worlds, "Water and fire to sell", are frequently observed. At these humble establishments boiling water and red-hot turf are sold to the poorer classes for the preparation of their tea or coffee. Many of the houses and public buildings are considerably out of perpendicular, a circumstance due to the soft and yielding nature of the ground on which they stand.

A SQARE IN UTRECHT, HOLLAND.—The name of this city is unquestionably a corruption of Oude Trecht, the translation of which is "old ford". It is one of the most ancient towns in the netherlands. At Utrecht the Rhine divides into two branches, one of which, named the Old Rhine, falls into the North sea, while the other, called the Vecht, empties itself into the Zuider Zee. The town is intersected by two canals which float far below the level of the adjoining houses; some of the rooms and vaults below the wharfs are occupied as dwellings. The archbishops of Utrecht were among the most powerful of the prelates of the middle ages, and the town was celebrated at an early period for the beauty of its churches. It first belonged to Lorraine and subsequently to the German empire, and was frequently the residence of the German emperor. The Emperor Conrad II died here in 1039. Adrian Bolyens, the tutor of Charles V, and one of the most pious and learned men of his age, afterward Pope Adrian VI, was born at Utrecht in 1459. In 1579 the union of the seven provinces of Holland, Zealand, Utrecht, Guelders, Overyssel, Freisland and Groningen, whereby the independence of the Netherlands was established, was concluded in the hall of the academy of Utrecht under the presidency of Count John, of Nassau, brother of William the Silent.

CITY OF BOMBAY, INDIA.—In natural scenery and in the advantages of its position, Bombay ranks first among the cities of India. The Bombay island stands out from the coast, ennobled by lofty mountains, and its harbor is studded by rock islands and precipices whose peaks rise to a great height. The approach from the sea discloses one of the finest panoramas in the world, the only European analogy being the Bay of Naples. The town itself consists of well-built and unusually handsome native bazaars and of spacious streets devoted to European commerce. In the native bazaar the houses rise three or four stories in height, with elaborately carved pillars and fretwork. Some of the hotels and other buildings are on the American scale and have no rival in any other city in India. Great varieties of climate are to be met with in Bombay. In its extremed dryness and heat portions of the country resemble the sultry deserts of Africa, the temperature averaging during six months of the year one hundred degrees in the shade, and the water of some of the rivers reaching blood heat. In Upper Sindh it is even hotter, and the thermometer has been known to register one hundred and thirty in the shade. The defenses of the port of Bombay consist chiefly in ironclad monitors anchored off the town, and one or two fortified islands. The Bombay island passed to the English crown as part of the dower of Princess Catherine.

CITY OF CALCUTTA, INDIA.—This glorious old city, the capital of India and seat of the supreme government, is situated on the bank of the Hugli river, about eighty miles from the seaboard, and receives the accumulated produce of which the two great river systems of the Ganges and the Brahmaputra collect throughout the provinces of Bengal and Assam. From a cluster of mud villages at the close of the last century, it has advanced with a rapid growth to the densely inhabited metropolis it now is, containing a population of nearly one million people. It grew without any fixed plan, and with little regard to the sanitary arrangments required for the town it was destined to be. Some parts of it lie below water, lying on the river, and the low level throughout renders its drainage a most difficult problem. The chief event in the history of Calcutta is the sack of the town and the capture of Fort William in 1756. The majority of the English officers took vessel and fled to the mouth of the river. The Europeans who remained were captured after a short resistance, and the prisoners, numbering about one hundred and fifty people, were driven at the point of the sword into the guard-room, a chamber scarcely twenty feet square, with but two small windows. Next morning only twenty-three were taken out alive, this circumstance giving rise to the remark relative to this fact of the "Black hole of Calcutta".

VIEW OF AMALFI, ITALY.—Amalfi is a lively town whose inhabitants' chief occupation is the manufacture of paper, soap and macaroni. The town is situated at the entrance of a deep ravine, surrounded by mountains and rocks of the most picturesque form. In the early part of the middle ages it was a propserous seaport, rivaling Pisa and Genoa. Amalfi is mentioned in history for the first time in the sixth century, when it enjoyed the protection of the Italian empire; it afterward became an independent state under the presidency. The town was at continued variance with the neighboring princes and even defied the gallant sovereign of Naples until King Roger conquered the place in 1131. United with the royal forces, Amalfi carried on a war with the Pisans; it was during this struggle that the celebrated manuscript of the "Pandects and Justimen" (which is now one of the principal treasures of the Laurentian Library at Florence) fell into the hand of the Pisans. The place then became subject to the king of the house of Aragon. In the twelfth century the sea began gradually to undermine the lower part of the town, and a terrible inundation in 1343 proved most disastrous. The town boasts of having given birth to Flavio Gioja, who invented the compass in the year 1302. The "Taval Amalfitane" were recognized for centuries as the maritime law of the Mediterranean.

THE PITTI PALACE, FLORENCE, ITALY.—This building stands conspicuously on an eminence, and was built in 1440 by the Pitti family, who hoped to excel in external grandeur, by the erection of the most imposing palace yet built be a private citizen, their powerful opponents, the Medici family. The failure of a conspiracy against Medici caused Pitti the loss of his power and influence, and the building remained unfinished for over a century, after which it was completed. The palace, which somewhat resembles a castle or a prison, is nevertheless remarkable for its bold simplicity, the unadorned blocks of stone being hewn smooth at the joints only. The central part has a third story. The effect of the building is entirely produced by its fine proportions, the total length being four hundred and seventy-five feet and its height one hundred and fourteen feet. Since the sixteenth century the Pitti palace has been the residence of the reigning sovereign of Italy, and is now occupied by King Humbert when at Florence. The upper floor contains the far-famed "Pitti Gallery", which has about five hundred paintings, and may be regarded as an extension of the Tribuna in the Uffizi gallery. No collection in Italy can boast of such an array of masterpieces. The treasures of the gallery culminate in Raphael's works, the best known of which is "The Madonna", a beautiful work which captivates every beholder.

THE CITY OF GENOA, ITALY.—Genoa is the chief commercial city of italy. Its situation rising above the sea in a wide semi-circle, and its numerous palaces justly entitle it to the ephithet of "The superb". The town is surrounded by extensive fortifications which date from the beginning of the seventeenth century, and have been recently materially strengthened. The heights around the town are crowned with ten detached turrets. The harbor consists of a semi-circular bay about four miles in length, protected from the open sea by long and substantial piers, the Duke of Galliera having presented four million dallors for its improvement on condition that the government and the city would complete the required sum. An outer basin, a new harbor and an inner basin have recently been constructed. From the earliest time Genoa has been famous as a seaport. The Roman form of its municipal government was maintained throughout the period of the barbarian invasions, when a new feudal nobility sprang up alongside the native nobles. The smaller towns on the coast looked upon Genoa as their champion against the Saracens, who ravaged the country, and in 936 even plundered Genoa itself. In 1015 the Genoans made themselves masters of Corsica, and in 1119 they waged a victorious war against Pisa. From that date the rival cities were almost permanently at war down to 1284, when the Pisans were conquered.

PANORAMA OF NAPLES.—The city of Naples, capital of the former kingdom of Naples, is now the most populous town in southern Italy and occupies one of the most beautfiful situations in the world. Its magnificent bay has from the most ancient times been the object of enthusiastic admiration, and it is annually visited by thousands of strangers in quest of enjoyment or health. Nature, it would appear, has so bountifully lavished her gifts on this favored spot that the energy and strength of the most powerful nations have invariably succumbed to its benign influence. Greeks, Romans, the French, Germans and Spaniards have in succession been masters of this place, yet it has rarely attained even a transient reputation in the annals of politics, art or literature. Scholars who recognized in Florence the focus of Italian art, in Rome the metropolis of the bygone ages, in Venice and Genoa the splendor of vanished republics can not but experience a feeling of disappointment on beholding Naples. The dearth of handsome buildings and indigenous works of art create a void for which the near by Herculaneum and Pompeii with their matchless treasures of antiquity alone, in some measure, compensate. The domestic architecture in the older part of Naples, the narrow dingy streets, the high and narrow houses with flat roofs and balconies in front of every window, are, it is true, attractive to strangers.

A STREET SCENE IN NAPLES.—The life of the people in Naples is carried on with greater freedom and more careless indifference to publicity than any other city in Europe. From morning till night the streets resound with the cries of the vendors of food and other articles; strangers are beset by swarms of peddlers pushing their wares and all eager and able to take advantage of the inexperience of their victims. At early hours the news vendor makes himself heard, and in the evening appear the lanterns of those who make a living hunting for cigar ends and similar unconsidered trifles. A double row of awnings stretch in front of the houses, under which cooks set up their portable stoves and drive a brisk trade in fish, meat or macaroni, while other dealers tempt the crowd with trays of carefully assorted cigar ends. The narrow streets, especially in the forenoon, afford a most characteristic study of the humbler city life. Every Monday and Friday there is a curious and animated rag fair, where all kinds of old clothes change hands. Public readers are also to be seem regularly about 4 P.M. Quack doctors extol their nostrums with interminable harangues which they punctuate by pulling teeth, and often a funeral procession passes escorted by the fantastically disguished members of the brotherhood to which the deceased has belonged.

THE SPANISH STEPS, ROME.—The long "Scala di Spagna", or Spanish steps, which descend from the Church of Trinity to the Piazza di Spagna by one hundred and thirty-five steps, was constructed in 1721. The Piazza di Spagna, at the foot of these steps, is the center of the strangers' quarters in Rome, and is enclosed by hotels and attractive stores. It is the custom for models for artists, dressed in their picturesque costumes, to frequent the vicinity of these steps, it not being an unusual sight to see from twenty to fifty of them picturesquely grouped, waiting the calls of artists that they may secure an engagement. On the left of the steps is the house in which John Keats died in 1821. The more remote history of Italy is enveloped in much obscurity, and so also the origin of the city of Rome is to a great extent a matter of conjecture. It was not until a comparatively late period that the legend of Romulus and Remus was framed, and the year B.C. 753 fixed as the date of foundation. Rome, unquestionably, however, may lay claim to far greater antiquity. The rapid recent growth of the city is mainly to be attributed to its situation, the most central in the peninsula, alike adapted for the great commerical town and for the capital of a vast empire. The Tiber was navigable for sea-going ships as far as Rome, during the ancient times, but is now navigable only for a short distance from its mouth.

GENERAL VIEW OF SYRACUSE, ITALY.—This town, which was in ancient time the most important one in Sicily, is situated on an island close to the Italian coast. It is one of the most interesting points in Sicily, its natural beauties vying with its great classical attractions. It was founded in 734 by Corinthians on the island where a Phoenician settlement had been established at an earlier period. The inhabitants were reduced to the condition of serfs and compelled to cultivate the soil, the government being conducted by the aristocracy, the descendants of the founders. Owing to the fertility of the soil the colony rapidly rose to prosperity. Syracuse was afterward reduced to great extremities by the Athenians, who in 415 B.C. sent a fleet of one hundred and thirty-four vessels to Sicily, hoping to conquer the island and thus extend their supremacy over the western Mediterranean. The Athenians were successful, and after their conquest, an enormous booty comprising valuable works of art was conveyed to Rome, and Syracuse sank to the condition of a Roman provincial town. Cicero described it as the largest of the Greek and the most beautiful of all cities. The present town occupies an island which forms but a small part of the site of the ancient city. The extremity of the island is protected by fortifications. The town is well supplied with modern improvements.

BRIDGE OF SIGHS, VENICE.—Mr. W.D. Howells, the well-known American author, calls the here pictured bridge a "pathetic swindle", and in reality too much sympathy need not be wasted on the bridge, as the present structure has sarcely ever felt the foot of a prisoner. The prisons under the leaden roof of the palace from which this bridge leads were destroyed in 1797. The series of gloomy dungeons, with a torture chamber and the place of execution for political criminals, have recently been made accessible to the general public. Admitting that it is a fact that too much sympathy has been spent on this bridge, it is also a fact that to separate all the romance from it is to remove one of the joys of a visit to Venice. The interior of the bridge is gloomy enough to start any creepy feeling one may have worked themselves up to. The council of Ten, or guardians of the public welfare in the middle ages in Venice, were supposed to have sent their condemned prisoners over this bridge, through the windows of which they obtained their last sight of the heavens. The standpoint from which this view is taken is a bridge leading to a dock paved with marble. This quay presents a busy scene, being the most popular lounge in Venice. The bridge from which this picture is taken leads to the walk where Shakespeare makes Shylock hold his conversation with Antonio.

THE GRAND CANAL, VENICE.—The Grand Canal in Venice is the main artery of the traffic of this wonderful city, and is nearly two miles in length with a breadth varying from one hundred to two hundred feet. It intersects the city from the northwest to the southeast, dividing it into two unique parts and resembles an inverted "S" in shape. Steam barges and hundreds of gondolas and other craft are to be seen during "the season", gliding upon it in every direction. Handsome houses and magnificent palaces rise on its banks, for this is the city of the nobility, the ancient aristocracy of Venice. A trip on the canal is always extrememly interesting. To the left in this picture on the point with a dome rises the principal custom-house erected in 1682, the vane of the tower of which has a gilt "Fortuna". The gondola takes the place of the cab at Venice. They are painted black in conformity with a law passed in the fifteenth century. The heavy iron prow is partly intended to counterbalance the weight of the rower who stands at the stern of the boat, and partly as a measure of the height of the bridges which can not be passed under unless the prow, which is the highest point of the craft, clears them. Gondolas with a gondolier can be hired for the first hour for twenty cents, and for each additional hour ten cents, or, by the whole day of ten hours, one dollar.

CITY AND HARBOR OF NAGASAKI.—Japan has been most jealous of foreign invasion up to quite a recent date. This is the well-known harbor of Nagasaki, to which foreign vessels have access and is the best known by name of all the open ports. It is situated in the province of Hizen in the large southwestern portion of Kiushui, the foreign settlement in which is small though the native town is of considerable extent. The principal export is coal. The number of large harbors and trade ports in Japan is stated to be fifty-six, but many of these would no doubt be inaccesible to foreign vessels of heavy tonnage; they are, however, admirably adapted for the accommodation of coasting junks and fishing craft, and these vessels have no lack of places of refuge in stormy weather. In many instances the entrances are blocked by one or more small islands or rocks which render the anchorage within even more secure. The Japanese, strange to say, have no name for either their bays or their straits, the names found on maps and charts having been given by European navigators. Rural life in Japan is of a nature to distress those who are accustomed to seeing the manner in which rural people live in other countries. Even the women and children go out to till the ground from early morn to late in the evening, their labor being sometimes varied by felling trees or cutting brush wood on the hills.

ISLAND OF MADEIRA.—This island, perhaps best known as producing the wine that is famous the world over, is one of a group of islands in the North Atlantic ocean that belong to Portugal, consisting of two inhabited islands named Madeira and Porto Santo and three uninhabited rocks named the Desartes. Funchal, here pictured, is the capital of Madeira. The island lies about three hundred and sixty miles from the coast of France, five hundred and thirty-five miles from Lisbon and four hundred and eighty from Santa Maria, the nearest of the Azores. The city is connected by submarine telegraph with Lisbon and Brazil. Madeira, the largest island of the group, has a length of thirty miles and extreme breadth of thirteen miles and a coast line of eighty or ninety miles. It is traversed by a mountain chain, having a main altitude of four thousand feet, up which many deep ravines penetrate from both coasts, rendering travel by land from place to place a very arduous and fatiguing task. The depth and narrowness of the ravines, the loftiness of the rugged peaks that tower above them, the bold precipices of the coast and the proximity of the sea afford many scenes of picturesque beauty and striking grandeur, which are continually changing character as the traveler advances on his way.

THE FAMOUS WAR-SCARRED CASTLE OF CHAPULTEPEC, MEXICO.—A sight of this castle is one of the anticipated pleasures of all Mexican tourists, and to gain admission (which can only be obtained during the winter season, as the president of the republic occupies it as a residence during the summer months), an order must be secured from the governor of the federal district. After a ride of about two miles from the City of Mexico over the magnificent boulevard drive of the city, Chapultepec is reached. This palace was for a time occupied by the unfortunate Maximilian and his faithful wife, Carlotta. A great traveler, in speaking of the charming valley which is seen from this castle, said: "I have seen the Simplon, the Spleugen, the view from Rhegi, the wide and winding Rhine and the prospect from Vesuvius over the lovely bay of Naples, its indolent waves sleeping in the warm sunlight of its purple bed, but none of these scenes compare with the valley at Mexico; they want some of the elements of grandeur, all of which are gathered here." The park which surrounds the castle is a charming spot. A short distance in the rear of the castle is Molino del Rey, the scene of the great Mexican war of 1847. General Grant, at that time lieutenant, was the first man to enter the mill after its capture.

THE CATHEDRAL, CITY OF MEXICO.—In the city of Mexico is the here pictured cathedral, which is Mexico's most famous structure. The building of this immense cathedral was begun in 1573 on the site of the greatest Aztec toecalli. Its cost was two million dollars. It is four hundred and twenty-six feet long, two hundred feet wide and the towers are two hundred and three feet from the pavement and were finished in 1791 at a cost of one hundred and ninety thousand dollars. The church contains five naves, six altars, fourteen chapels and two very large organs. Several rich Spaniards donated costly vessels of gold, silver and precious stones worth one million, eight hundred and fifty thousand dollars for the interior decoration of this cathedral. The adventurous mining king, José Borda, presented a chalice covered with thousands of diamonds which cost him three hundred thousand dollars, but after his bankruptcy he asked for a gratifiction and received payment of one-third of the value. These jewels are not now in the church, having been sequestered by the goverment of Juarez. The facade, with its combination of gray sandstone and white marble, presents a very pleasing effect. The central portion, gradually rising, is divided by prodigious buttresses into three turrets of various orders of architecture. In the west tower hangs a large bell measuring sixteen and one-half feet high.

THE NATIONAL PALACE, CITY OF MEXICO.—This is the largest building in Mexico and occupies a block or square of five hundred and ninety feet. The facade with its square cornered tower, the embattled roof and the iron grating before the windows, remind one more of a prison or barrack than a palace. The building has gradually grown to that planless architectural monstrosity which it now represents. It contains twelve court-yards of various sizes, around which the buildings are grouped. In 1592 the government bought the building that occupied this site of the heirs of Cortez for thirty-five thousand dollars, but in the riots of 1692 it was totally destroyed. The present building was completed in 1699. It contains the official residence of the President of Mexico, the departments of interior, of war, finance, senate chamber, general post office and other public offices. Above the central doorway is a clock which was exiled from a Spanish village for once having caused great alarm there by striking of its own accord. If permission is granted the traveler to see the National Palace, he is accompanied by an officer or employe up the main stairs to the upper story from which he descends, visiting all the rooms of interest on the way down. To see the presidential apartments a special permit is necessary, which is granted to visitors only when the president is absent and is to be obtained on personal application.

THE CITY OF VERA CRUZ, MEXICO.—It is hardly necessary to refer to the remarkable attractiveness of Mexico and how decidedly prominent and popular that country has become as a tourist resort within the past few years, for able writers have sounded its praises far and wide. It is the "wonderland" on the American continent. The magnificent harbor here pictured is one that any city or country might be glad to possess, as it has few equals; the style of the typical Mexican building is also shown here to the very best advantage. Prescott, in the opening paragraph of his "Conquest of Mexico", says: "Of all that extensive empire which once acknowledged the authority of Spain in the New World, no portion for interest and importance can be compared with Mexico, and this equally, whether we consider the quality of its soil and climate, the inexhaustible sources of its mineral wealth, its scenery grand and picturesque beyond example, the character of its ancient inhabitants, or the peculiar circumstances of its conquest, adventurous and remarkable as any legend devised by Norman or Italian bard of chivalry." It should be remembered that Cortez invaded Mexico only twenty-seven years following the discovery of America, and yet he found a people proficient in stone carving and other works of art, and with a government at whose head was Montezuma, that considerably antedated the landing of Columbus.

THE CASINO AT MONTE CARLO.—The town of Monte Carlo is a health resort in winter and a sea bathing place in the summer, but the chief attraction to many visitors is the opportunity presented for gambling at the here pictured Casino, which stands on a rocky promontory to the east end of the town in beautiful grounds commanding a fine view. The establishment is most luxuriantly fitted up, and is adorned with works of art. Tickets of admission are supplied gratis on presenting an individual visiting card at the office in the vestibule. The doors of this famous gambling establishment open three hundred and sixty-five times a year, Sundays, holidays and all other days, at twelve o'clock noon, and close promptly at twelve midnight. Before the doors open, the crowd surrounding them can be seen, eager to get first admission for the purpose of securing a seat at one of the tables, there being room for only sixteen players at each table, and it not being an unusual occurrence for others, anxious to put their money on the table, to stand three or four deep behind those seated, scrambling for an opportunity to get his or her money, as the case may be, on the green cloth before the ball drops. The only restrictions against an entrance to the Casino are, youth and a permanent residence in the principality of Monaco. The proprietors know only too well the effect of gaming on those who become infatuated, and consequently refuse to allow their neighbors to participate.

QUEEN STREET, AUCKLAND, NEW ZEALAND.—New Zealand is so far away that it is a terra incognito to most Americans, to whom it may be a surprise to know that the city of Auckland is as well supplied with modern conveniences as is any American city of equal population. Auckland is the capital of the province or county of the same name and is finely situated on the shore of as good a harbor as New Zealand possesses. The city was founded in 1840 by Governor Hobson. The city has a fine appearance, especially from the harbor, and is surrounded by numerous suburban villages, with which it is connected by railways. Among its fine public edifices may be mentioned the governor's house, the cathedral, St. John's college and others. The first European discoverer of New Zealand was Tasman, after whom Tasmania is named. Captain Cook afterward visited the island and took possession of it for Great Britain. He introduced several useful animals and plants which afterward increased and multiplied until now New Zealand mutton is one of the chief staple food supplies in England, to which country it is exported in millions of tons annually in vessels specially fitted for that trade. Something like twenty million dollars' worth of wool is also annually exported. Sheep shipped to England net the shippers about five dollars and twenty-five cents each.

THE CATHEDRAL OF LIMA, PERU.—The Cathedral, which may be termed the most imposing edifice of picturesque Lima if not of Peru, is built of adobe brick, mud, mortar, broken stone, bamboo cane and timber, covered over with salmon coloured stucco. The facade, flanked on either side by towers after the Tuscan style, is twelve meters long and fifty meters in height. Ten board steps the entire width of the building lead to the main entrance, the center door of which is known as the "Door of Pardon"; like the other doors of the building it is studded with large Moorish nails. Above the Gothic arch are a series of galleries supported by light Corinthian columns, exquisitely carved; these columns define the niches, placed one above the other, on either side of the door, in which are the statues of Saints Matthew, Mark, Luke and Jerome. Above this arch is a statue of the Virgin, between Saints Peter and Paul, surmounted by one of Santo Toribio, blessing a kneeling Indian, over whom is suspended the Imperial Arms of Charles V. Upon the apex of the arched front is a pedestal upon which stands John the Evangelist blessing the Cathedral. The other two doors, a mixture of Corinthian and Doric, have little ornamentation except the Corinthian columns, which support the arches and form the niches in which stand two other statues.

CHURCH AND CONVENT OF SAN FRANCISCO, LIMA, PERU.—The church and adjoining convent of San Francisco, in Lima, Peru, forms an immense pile on the Plaza Mayor and in the vicinity of the Rimac, which flows through the city. It is said to be the most extensive and costly in Lima. The style is composite Moorish and the ornamentation elaborate. Like all the old buildings of Peru, the material is of brick, broken stone, mortar and plaster covered with stucco and painted. The domes are of geometrical design and are composed of pieces of wood joined together with groove and slot, and finished after the manner of the domes and ceiling of the Alhambra and of the Alcazar in Seville; the belfries and turrets are of timber and cane finished with stucco moldings. The facade is pitted with bullet holes, but the towers have suffered worst of all; from one of the towers projects a beam from which more than one unsuccessful political aspirant has been hung and left to rot. During one of the revolutions a leader took refuge in one of these turrets and was bombarded by the occupants of the Casa Verde. The interiors of the church and convent are covered with beautiful tiles, which have withstood earthquakes, revolutions and the test of centuries; they are celebrated for their fine quality, exquisite design and lustre; these tiles cover many acres of surface and are said to have been unsurpassed by any similar product of modern times.

100

THE CITY OF LISBON, PORTUGAL.–This city is the capital of the kingdom of Portugal, and is located on the banks of the Tagus, at a spot where the river broadens to the width of nine miles, some eight or nine miles from the point where enters the Atlantic ocean. Standing on a low range of hills backed by lofty granite mountains, and extending along the margin of the wide Tagus, Lisbon presents a noble aspect to those who approach it from the sea. In regard to the beauty of its position, it may rightly claim to be the third of the European cities, Constantinople and Naples alone ranking before it. The river affords secure anchorage for a very large number of vessels, and the bar at the mouth is easily crossed even in rough weather. Lisbon projects along the mouth of the river for four or five miles, and extends backward over the hills for nearly three miles, but much of it is scattered among gardens and fields. In the older part the streets are very irregular, but that portion which was rebuilt after the great earthquake of 1755 consists of lofty houses ranged in long, straight streets. By far the most interesting object architecturally in Lisbon is its cathedral, which was begun in 1500, near the spot where Vasco de Gama had embarked three years before on his famous voyage to India. The style is a curious mixture of Moorish-Gothic and Renaissance styles with magnificent details.

101

THE PLACE OF COMMERCE, LISBON.—Here is pictured one of the four principal squares in the city of Lisbon and the foremost of them all. It is open one side to the river, and the other three sides are surrounded by the custom house and government offices with spacious arcades beneath. In the middle is a bronze equestrian statue of Joseph I, in whose reign the earthquake and restoration of the city took place. At the middle of the north side is a grand triumphal arch, under which is a street leading to another handshome square, the Place Dom Pedro, of which this book also contains a photograph. When the city of Lisbon was destroyed in 1755, the earthquake took place in the bottom of the sea fifty miles west of the city, yet it so agitated the water that a wave sixty feet high dashed over Lisbon, destroying it and its inhabitants in a space of six minutes. Its houses are for the most part well built, and are divided into flats for the accommodation of several families. The streets formerly had a bad reputation in regard to cleanliness, but of late years great improvment has taken place in this respect, although no general system of drainage has yet been adopted. The city contains seven theatres and a bullring. The hotels of Lisbon offer but indifferent accommodations to strangers and the shops present little display, being but poorly furnished with wares.

PLACE DOM PEDRO, LISBON.—The beauties of the city of Lisbon are not only in its situation, which all admit is the most charming one, but also in its squares or open places. The one here pictured is that known as the Place Dom Pedro, and occupies the site of the old palace and prisons of the Inquisition, the establishment of which was accomplished as follows: The great discoveries of the fifteenth century weakened the population of Portugal; whole families migrated to Madeira and the Brazils, and the bulk of young men volunteered as soldiers and sailors to go in search of wealth and honor; also, the Portuguese who did continue to live in their native country flocked to Lisbon, which trebled in population in less than eighty years, owing to the large fortunes which could be made there in commercial pursuits. The king and nobles were quite unconcerned at this extensive emigration, for their large estates were cultivated much more cheaply by African slaves, who were imported in such number that even in Lisbon itself they outnumbered the free men. While the Portuguese nation was exhibiting these signs of rapid decline, a factor was added by the religious zeal of John III. This king first fostered bigotry and fanaticism, and eventually succeeded in introducing the Jesuits and the Inquisition into Portugal, he executing his object with the aid of the Church of Rome in 1536.

THE KREMLIN IN MOSCOW.—Russian antiquarians are unable to trace the name of the Kremlin to any certain source. The principal portion of the Kremlin is the here photographed "Tower of Ivan the Great". Tradition points to a very remote origin for this remarkable structure, but historical facts assert that it was built in the year 1600. It consists of five stories, the whole rising to a height of about three hundred and twenty-five feet, including the cross, which has been set up since 1812, in place of the one which Napoleon removed, under the impression that it was of great value, whereas it had cost only five thousand dollars. As one gazes on the Kremlin he pictures to himself what must have been the feelings of the French army when they caught the first glimpse of its golden minarets and starry towers. After traversing the dreary plains with fearful loss and fighting their way up to this spot, the limit of their long career, no wonder that those weary legions, led by Napoleon, were unable to suppress their joy and shouted with one voice, "Moscow!" The great bell of Moscow lies at the foot of the tower. Its weight at present is four hundred and forty thousand pounds; its height from the top of the bell to the cross placed upon it by the order of Emperor Nicholas I, is twenty-six feet four inches, and its circumference sixty-seven feet eleven inches. It is two feet thick, and the weight of the broken piece, eleven tons.

ROYAL PALACE OF PETERHOF, NEAR ST. PETERSBURG.–The construction of this prettily situated palace was commenced about 1720. The building is situated at an elevation of sixty feet, and was built under the direction of Peter the Great. Although other emperors and empresses made alterations and additions, the character of the whole is the same as that of all the palaces built by Peter the Great. Inside are to be seen some beautiful tapestry, countless articles of vertu and numbers of excellent paintings. There is also one highly interesting apartment containing a collection of eight hundred and sixty-three female portraits, executed for Empress Catherine during a visit, which the artist made to fifty provinces of Russia. They are all portraits of beautiful young girls, painted in picturesque attitudes, in their national costumes. The garden surrounding the palace is laid out in terrces, adorned with fountains and waterfalls. The waterworks are considered equal in all respects to those at Versailles, France. The fountain called the "Samson", in front of the palace, is a magnificent jet of water which rushes to a height of eighty feet. On each side of the Samson (so called from the colossal bronze figure tearing open the jaws of the lion) are other jets which throw water vertically and horizontally. These basins are at the foot of the elevation on which the palace stands.

THE HERMITAGE, ST. PETERSBURG.—This wonderful gallery and museum, which contains one of the most extensive modern collections, was founded by Catherine the Great. It was intended by the empress as a refuge from the courts and duties of government, and hence was called the Hermitage. Her leisure moments and her evenings were spent there in conversation with philosophers, men of letters and artists. For elegance, purity of architectural forms and the variety as well as costliness of the metals employed, this museum has scarcely any equal in Europe. At the door of one of the rooms in the Romanoff gallery in St. Petersburg a green curtain drawn over a tablet conceals the rules which the Empress Catherine enforced at her conversaziones in the Hermitage. The following is a translation of those rules: 1. Leave your rank outside, as well as your hat, and especially your sword. 2. Leave your right of precedence, your pride, and any similar feeling, outside the door. 3. Be gay, but do not spoil anything; do not break or *gnaw* anything. 4. Sit, stand, walk as you will, without reference to anybody. 5. Talk moderately and not very loud, so as not to make the ears and heads of others ache. 6. Argue without anger and without excitement. 7. Neither sigh nor yawn, nor make anybody dull or heavy. 8. In all innocent games, whatever one proposes, let all join. 9. Eat whatever is sweet and savory, but drink with moderation, so that each may find his legs on leaving the room. 10. Tell no tales out of school; whatever goes in at one ear must go out at the other before leaving the room.

LADY KAZAN CATHEDRAL. ST. PETERSBURG.—This church stands on the Nevski Prospect, St. Petersburg's most famous street. A comparison is at once made with the building in consequence of its colannade being an imitation of St. Petersburg at Rome. It was founded in 1802 and consecrated in 1811, after an outlay of about three million dollars. Built on piles, it has the shape of a cross with a length of two hundred and eighty feet between its extremities, and a breadth of one hundred and eighty-two feet. The cupola and cross rises more than two hundred and thirty feet above the ground. Inside the church a colonnade extends in four rows from the four pillars which support the cupola toward the altar and the three principal doors of the cathedral. It consists of fifty-six monoliths of Finland granite thirty-five feet in height, rising on bronze bases and terminating in Corinthian capitals in the same metal. The altar is of silver, as is also the balustrade in front of it. An inscription on it states that the silver of which it was made was the zealous offering of the Don Cossacks, after the campaign of 1812. The name of the altar is rendered in precious stones in the center of the upper door of the screen. The miraculous image of the Virgin, brought from Kazan in 1579 and removed to St. Petersburg in 1821, is in the altar, covered with fine gold and precious stones, valued at more than seventy-five thousand dollars.

ST. ISAAC'S CATHEDRAL, ST. PETERSBURG.—This edifice can not fail to excite the admiration of those who appreciate grand proportions, a simple but lofty style of architecture and noble porticoes. Its situation is highly suitable, notwithstanding the low elevation of the ground at St. Petersburg, for it occupies one of the largest open spaces in the Russian capital. Being surrounded by its finest buildings and monuments, it gives the stranger some idea of what Russian quarries, mines and workmen can produce. Nothing can exceed the simplicity of the building; no ornamentation meets the eye, the architect having left all to the impression to be produced by gigantic proportions and excellence of material. On the spot where the cathedral stands the Russians had been at work upon a place of worship for an entire century. The original church was of wood, and constructed by Peter the Great, in 1710, but this was subsequently destroyed, and the great Catherine commenced another, which was finished in 1801. This edifice vanished in its turn, and the present magnificent structure was commenced in 1819, and occupied thrity-nine years in construction. In order to make a firm foundation a whole forest of piles, twenty-one feet in length, was sunk in the swampy soil at a cost of one million dollars. The cost of this cathedral was $15,000,000, an equivalent to the cost of the Brooklyn Bridge.

STATUE OF PETER THE GREAT, ST. PETERSBURG.—This statue ranks first among the monuments of St. Petersburg. It stands opposite the St. Isaac's cathedral close to the River Neva. The whole group was produced at a single casting by Falconet. The arrangement of the head of the emperor, which is said to be a striking likeness of Peter, was modeled by Mary Callot, who subsequently became the wife of the designer of the statue. The emperor is admirably represented reigning in his horse on the brink of a rock, on both sides of which, as well as in front, is a precipice threatening immediate destruction. His face is turned toward the river, his outstretched hand pointing to the result of his thought and will, while a serpent, emblematical of difficulties which Peter encountered in building St. Petersburg, is trodden under foot by the spirited horse. The whole is wonderfully balanced on the hanging rock, and the tail of the horse, which is joined to the serpent's body, and into which ten thousand pounds of metal have been thrown (the entire weight of the metal being about sixteen tons) has been so skilfully distributed by varying the thickness of the bronze from one inch to one-quarter of an inch in thickness, that the center of gravity is fixed immediately above the horse's hoofs, which rest on the rock.

WINTER PALACE, ST. PETERSBURG.—The here pictured palace is that of the residence of the Czar of Russia and his court during the winter season, and stands on the site of a house which in the reign of Peter the Great belonged to his high admiral. The building has been the scene of several serious conflagrations, from which in 1839 it was entirely restored. The huge pile is about eighty feet high, the frontage four hundred and fifty-five feet in length, and its depth three hundred and fifty feet. The most elegant and glittering apartment of this palace is the drawing-room of the empress. The light of day can, however, scarcely do justice to all the magnificence which is here to be seen. No court in Europe presents such a brilliant appearance as that of Russia when seen in the Winter Palace.

The Alexander column which is to be seen in front of the palace is the greatest monolith of modern times. It is eighty-four feet in height, but originally measured one hundred and two feet, having been subsequently shortened from the fear that its diameter of eleven feet was insufficient for so great a length. As the whole of St. Petersburg is built on a marsh, it was found necessary to drive no fewer than six successive rows of piles in order to sustain its immense weight; and the shaft of the column alone is commputed to weigh nearly four hundred tons, and the massive pedestal, which is seventy feet in height, materially increases the tremendous pressure.

THE ROYAL PALACE, HONOLULU, SANDWICH ISLANDS.—The here pictured building is that which was occupied by the Queen of the Sandwich Islands, who succeeded her brother, Kalakau. He was perhaps the best known in America of foreign potentates, having frequently made trips to the United States, and having as his chief advisors, Americans who had gone to his country to reside. When we consider that it was only in 1778 that these islands were discovered by Captain Cook, the strides made there in a little over one hundred years are phenomenal. On his first visit, Captain Cook was received by the natives with many demonstrations of astonishment and delight, and offerings were presented to him in one of the temples by their priests; although in the following year he was killed by a native when he landed on these islands. His bones were preserved by the priests and continued to receive offerings and homage from the people until the abolition of idolatry. At the time of Cook's visit, each of these islands had its chief. In 1820, missionaries from America commenced their labors at Honolulu, a short time prior to which idolatry and worship of images had been abolished by the reigning sovereign. In the former state of things, the people were extremely licentious; men were living with several wives, and women were living with several husbands. Virtue was an unknown thing, there being no native word for it.

111

PRINCES STREET AND SCOTT MONUMENT, EDINBURGH.–Princes Street, the leading street of Edinburgh, is noted for its fine situation. One one side it is flanked by a row of magnificent buildings and attractive shops; on the other the eye wanders from the trim gardens adorned with monuments to the grim precipitous rock, whose ridge is appropriately crowned with Edinburgh Castle. The view to the east is closed by Calton Hill, which is surmounted with monuments. The most conspicuous monument in Princes Street Gardens is that of Sir Walter Scott. This was designed by G.M. Kemp, a self-taught architect who died before his design was realized, and consists of a Gothic spire two hundred feet in height.

A statue of the great novelist with his favorite dog beside him stands beneath the arch, and a stair leads to the gallery at the top, where a fine view of the city may be had. The monument is also enriched with thirty-two statuettes of the creations of the poet's imagination, among the subjects represented being "Meg Merriles", "The Lady of the Lake", "The Last Minstrel", and others. The narrow vale, of which Princes Street Gardens forms a part, was at one time a sheet of water called Nor' Loch. This was drained about the middle of the last century and the lower part of it is now the site of the great Waverly Railway Station.

THE CELEBRATED BRIDGE AT THE FRITH OF FORTH, SCOTLAND.—This structure was pronounced by M. Eiffel (who built the Eiffel Tower in Paris) to be the greatest construction in the world, and undoubtedly it is the most striking feature yet attained by engineering as applied to bridge-building. This wonderful bridge, the total length of which, including the approaches, is two thousand seven hundred and sixty-five yards, was begun in 1888 and finished seven years later at a cost of twelve and a half million dollars. It is built on the cantilever and central girder system, the working of which is that of stable equilibrium, its own weight helping to maintain it more firmly in position. Each of the main spans is seventeen hundred feet in length (or one hundred feet longer than the Brooklyn Bridge), and is formed of two cantilevers, each six hundred and eighty feet long, united by a girder three hundred and fifty feet long. The steel towers from which the cantilevers spring are three hundred and sixty feet high and are supported on granite piers. The clear headway at high-water is one hundred and fifty-one feet.

N.B. The spelling FRITH OF FORTH *is as it occurs in the original – possibly a typographical error.*

ST. GEORGE'S SQUARE, GLASGOW.—The square here pictured is in many senses the real center of this maritime Scotch city. One side of it is occupied by the North British Railway Station, another by the Bank of Scotland, a third by the general post-office, and the whole of the eastern side, the one here pictured, is occupied by the new municipal buildings, which are excedingly fine. The rapid growth of Glasgow is strikingly exemplified by the fact that no fewer than four times in the course of three-fourths of a century have the municipal authorities been obliged to seek new and enlarged accommodations for public offices. The designs of the buildings were by a native of Paisley, Scotland. In the center, near the grand entrance, rises a fine tower two hundred feet above the street level. A remarkable feature of the structure is the profuse employment of statuary groups and figures for its enrichment. Over two and a quarter million dollars were expended for the purchase of the site and the construction of the building. The square which it faces is the modern Walhalla of Glasgow, and contains numerous monumental erections and statues. The center is occupied by a fluted column with massive bases rising eighty feet, and surmounted with the colossal statue of Sir Walter Scott. Flanking it are equestrian bronze statues of Queen Victoria and her husband, also a statue of Robert Burns.

CITY OF MESSINA, SICILY.—Messina, next to Palermo, is the chief commercial town of Sicily. It is the seat of a Court of Appeals, an Archbishopric and a University, and is situated on the Straits of Messina. In grandeur of scenery it vies with Pisa. The harbor, which is formed by the peninsula, in the shape of a sickle, is the busiest in Italy, in point of steamboat traffic, and is one of the best in the world. It is entered annually by upward of four thousand large vessels, of which fully one-third are steamers. The climate of Messina is healthy, being neither cold in winter nor oppressively hot in summer, but the currents of air passing through the straits render it trying to consumptives or rheumatic persons. The town and environs present some excellent points of view, particularly toward Calabria by evening light, while the morning affords a strikingly grand survey of Mount Aetna and the blue mountains of Sicily. Messina has experienced long vicissitudes. It was founded by pirates in 72 B.C., and was called "Zankel" or Sickle, from the peculiar form of its harbor. About 493 B.C., inhabitants from all quarters settled in the city and gave it the name of Messina. During the eighteenth century Messina was overtaken by two overwhelming calamities—a fearful plague in 1740, by which forty thousand persons died, and an earthquake in 1783, which overthrew almost the whole town.

CITY OF PALERMO, SICILY.—The city here pictured is the capital of Sicily and contains a quarter of a million inhabitants, including the surrounding villages, and is the military, judiciary and ecclesiastical headquarters of the island on which it is located. It lies on the Bay of Palermo, which opens toward the sea, enclosed by fertile plains, beyond which rises an amphitheatre of grand mountains. Palermo is justly entitled to the ephithet "The beautiful", on account of its magnificent situation and delightful climate. The town is on a hill, well built, although the houses are generally of unimposing exterior. The commerce of the city, which is to a great extent in the hands of foreigners, has overtaken that of Messina and is steadily increasing. Sumach, oranges and lemons are largely exported. The harbor presents an animated scene, steamers of many foreign countries calling at its port. It was originally a Phoenician city, and, until it was captured in B.C. 254 by the Romans, was one of the most important strongholds of the Carthagenians. It was not until the fifteenth century that Palermo began to recover from the effects of a long period of anarchy under which it had been suffering. The Spanish viceroys selected this city as their residence and the nobles and ecclesiastics of their court contributed to its magnificence amd gayety. Palermo posseses very few ancient architectural remains.

THE ROYAL PALACE, MADRID.—It is becase Charles V suffered so much from the gout that Madrid was chosen as the capital of Spain. He found relief for his complaint from its sharp air, and it was thenceforth adopted as the home of royalty, although no situation can possibly be more odious to ordinary mortals. Situated twenty-four hundred feet above the sea, it has none of the advantages and all the disadvantages of a high position. The climate is burning hot in summer and piercingly cold in winter. All around the country is utterly barren and hideous; not a tree, not a drop of water, no green plants, not even a blade of grass, but only roads deep in dust; and the entire district is covered with brown sand or dull, gray rock. On the accession of Phillip III to the throne of Spain he desired to move the capital back to Seville, but it was then too late, partly because the building of the palace had added such a heavy link in the chain which bound the capital to Madrid. It is said that the air of Madrid is so subtle that it kills a man and does not put out a candle. A well-known writer, commenting on the place, says: "He who wishes for you does not know you; he who knows you does not wish for you"; and it certainly is a true proverb regarding the present royal city, yet the self-glorious Spaniards call theirs the only court, and believe that the world is silent and awed before its splendor.

CITY OF SEVILLE.—The people of Seville all seem proud now of its Moorish history and aware of the advantage which that period has bequeathed to them. All the best Moorish houses are preserved and the hot season of the "Oven of Spain", as Seville is called, is rendered endurable by the foresight which made the streets so narrow that it is generally impossible for two carriages to pass one another, while the houses which line them have large gardens or are built around upon courts, which in summer are covered with awnings, and the windows darkened by thick matted blinds. The names, which are written at the entrance of the streets in Seville, are in themselves picturesue and interesting, and have reference to events which occurred in them or persons who lived there. In the streets where most business is carried on, barriers are placed at each end of the broad flag pavements to prevent carriages from entering, so that only mules and donkeys jostle the foot passengers. If you turn into the quieter streets flanked by private houses, you may generally see scenes which look as if they were taken out of the play of Romeo and Juliet, of young men wrapped in their cloaks, clinging to the iron bars of one of the lower windows, making love. Only at Seville there is nothing surreptitious in this; it is the approved fashion, admitted by parents and guardians, and to neglect it on the part of the infatuated would be to forfeit his lady love's good graces.

GOTHENBURG, SWEDEN.—Gothenburg, a busy and prosperous commercial city, which has outstriped Stockholm in some respects, lies in an extensive plain on the left bank of the broad Götaelf, about five miles from its mouth, and has an excellent harbor, which is rarely blocked with ice. The town was founded in 1619 by Dutch settlers (including the wealthy Abraham Cabeliou), on the invitation of Gustavus Adolphus, who brought with them their national style of constructing streets and canals. The first great impulse to its commerce was given by the great continental blockade (1806), during which it formed the chief depot of the English trade with the north of Europe. It now owns a large commercial fleet and has world-wide business connections. Several of the chief merchants resident here are Scottish and German. The staple products are cotton, machinery, beer and sugar, and ship-building is largely carried on. With its suburbs, Gothenburg has now upward of one hundred thousand inhabitants.

THE STORA THEATRE, GOTHENBURG, SWEDEN.—The building here shown is a fine one in every respect and is admirably adapted to the uses for which it was constructed. It is situated in a city after which it was named, where the licensing system, which has given rise to so much controversy, has been in operation here for many years and has worked well. It is at least certain that drunkenness has diminished greatly of late years. The system was also introduced at Stockholm in October, 1877, and the results are said to have been beneficial. The leading features of the system of licensing, or rather of non-licensing, are that a company is empowered to buy up all licenses and existing rights, and to open a limited number of shops for the sale of pure and unadulterated spirits, the salaried managers of which have no interest whatever in the sale of the spirits. The company, which is under the supervision of the municipality, after deducting interest at the rate of five per cent. on the capital expended, hands over the whole of the surplus profits to the civic authorities, thus affording substantial relief to the rate-payers, and to some extent throwing the burden of maintaining the poor upon those who impoverish themselves by their own intemperance.

VIEW OF STOCKHOLM, SWEDEN.–Stockholm, the capital of the kingdom of Sweden, the seat of government and the supreme courts of law, lies at the influx of Lake Mälaren into an arm of the Baltic. It possesses excellent harbors, both in the Baltic and the Mälar, which present a lively scene, except when frozen over for four or five months in winter. The situation of the city on islands, on a plain and on rocky hills, surrounded by water in almost every direction, is highly picturesque. Stockholm has therefore been called the "Venice of the North", and has also been compared with Marseilles or Geneva; but no such comparison can convey an accurate idea of the place. Its most striking peculiarity consists in its immediate proximity with primeval forests and rocky islands, where to this day there is hardly a trace of cultivation. The foundation of Stockholm dates from Jarl Birger, of Bjelbo, who, in 1255, on the site of a settlement which had been repeatedly destroyed by pirates and hostile tribes (the Esthonians and Carelians, about the year 1188), fortified the islands now called Staden, Helgeandsholmen and Riddarholmen, with towers and walls, and made them the capital of his dominions. It was long before the city extended beyond these islands.

PALACE OF THE CROWN PRINCE, STOCKHOLM.—At the north end of the Norrbro, one of the islands comprising Stockholm's site, lies the Gustaf-Adolfs-Torg, or open space, in which rises a lofty pedestal of Swedish granite and marble bearing an equestrian statue of Gustavus Adolphus, in bronze, designed by L'Archevêque in 1777, and erected in 1796. The pedestal is adorned with bronze reliefs of the Swedish generals, Torstensson, Wrangel, Banér and Königsmark. On November 6th, the anniversary of the great king's death, the citizens crowd around the monument, singing national songs and the lines composed by Gustavus himself before the battle of Lützen ("Förfäras ej du lilla hop", "fear not, thou little band"). On the west side of the Gustaf-Adolfs-Torg, the building back of the monument, rises the palace of the crown prince, erected in 1783–93, now almost uninhabited. On the east side is the Stora Theater, designed by Adlercrantz, erected in 1775–82 by Gustavus III, and dedicated to "National Poetry", of which the king was an enthusiastic patron. Among the visitors at his court were Kellgrén, Lidner, Leopold and Bellman, the fathers of Swedish literature. It was in this theatre, at a masked ball on March 15–16, 1792, that Gustavus III was assassinated by Captain Ankarström.

RIDDARHOLMS CHURCH, STOCKHOLM.—The most prominent church in Sweden is the here pictured one with its conspicuous perforated spire of cast iron, two hundred and ninety feet high. It was formerly a church of the Franciscans, and has for centuries been the burial place of the Swedish kings and heroes. The building is Gothic disfigured by renaissance additions. Divine worship has not been performed here since 1807, except in the case of royal funerals. The principal entrance is at the west end. The walls of the church are blazoned with the armorial bearings of the deceased knights of the Seraphim Order and the pavement is formed of tombstones. Flanking the high altar are the monuments of Kings Magnus Ladulas (died 1320) and Charles VII (died 1470), erected in the reign of John III (sixteenth century). On the right (south) is the burial chapel of Gustavus Adolphus (*Gustavinska Grafkoret*), constructed in 1633, by order of the king in 1629, before his departure for Germany. Since 1832, the two hundredth anniversary of the famous monarch's death (at the battle of Lützen, November 6, 1632), his remains have reposed in a green marble sarcophagus, executed in Italy by order of Gustavus III, for the reception of the body of his father, Adolphus Frederick, but unused till 1832, when the remains of Gustavus Adolphus were transferred to it by Charles XIV, John.

ROYAL PALACE, STOCKHOLM, SWEDEN.—On the end of the island of Staden, one of the islands on which Stockholm is located, rises the here pictured royal palace, begun on the site of an earlier edifice by Nicodemus Tessin, a Swedish architect, in 1697, and in the Italian renaissance style. The work was interrupted by the wars of Charles XII, but was completed by Count Carl Gustavus Tessin, son of the first architect, Harlemann, and Cronstedt, in 1760. This spacious edifice, consisting of ground floor, entresol and two upper stories, with a flat roof, forms a rectangle one hundred and thirty-six yards by one hundred and twenty-seven yards, and encloses a court nearly square in shape. The north and south facades are adjoined by four lower wings, extending east and west, so that the north facade is double the length of the central building. The northwest portal, facing the bridge, has a handsome approach, constructed in 1824–34, and called "Lejonbacken", from the bronze lions, cast in 1704, which adorn it. On the southwest side of the palace are two detached buildings, forming a small semi-circular outer court, one of them being the chief guard-house. On the northeast side, between the projecting wings, is a small garden called Logarden or "lynx-yard", which is said to derive its name from a small menagerie once kept here. The central quadrangle is open to the public.

TOWN OF CHAMOUNIX, SWITZERLAND.—The valley of Chamounix, in which this town is situated, is about twelve miles long and half a mile wide and is bounded by the Mont Blanc chain with its huge ice cataracts and glaciers. A Benedictine priory first brought the valley into cultivation at the beginning of the twelfth century, but the reputation of the inhabitants was for a long period so bad that when the Bishop of Geneva, in 1622, visited the then pathless wilds on foot, his act was considered one of the utmost temerity. The valley became better known in 1743 when the celebrated traveler Pococke and a Mr. Windham visited and explored it in all directions and published their observations in the "Swiss Manual". Curiosity and enterprise were further stimulated by later publications of Swiss naturalists. Since that time Chamounix has become the great center of attraction for travelers, especially Americans, English and French, and is visited by upward of fiteen thousand people annually. It is inferior to the Bernese Oberland in picturesqueness of scenery, but superior in the grandeur of its glaciers, in which respect it has no rival. A peculiarity of the Alpine guide system is that travelers are provided with guides by the guide chef, the traveler having no choice except in rare cases, such as when ladies desire special guides, or travelers having had a guide desire to re-engage the same one.

125

CITY OF GENEVA, SWITZERLAND.—Geneva lies at an elevation of twelve hundred and forty-three feet and has a population of seventy-five thousand, including its suburbs. It is the largest and richest town in Switzerland, and lies at the south end of Lake Geneva at a point where the blue waters of the River Rhone emerge from it with the swiftness of an arrow. The Rhone divides the town into two parts, on the left bank of which lies the old town, the seat of government and the center of traffic. On the right is the Quartier St. Gervais, formerly a suburb. The old fortifications having been removed, the town has extended rapidly and new streets are still springing up. The famous Lake of Geneva has an extreme depth of one thousand and fifteen feet, and occupies an area of two hundred and twenty-five square miles, and in shape resembles a half moon with the horns extended to the south. The deep blue color of the lake differs from that of other Swiss lakes, which are all more or less of a greenish hue. The birds which haunt the lake are: Wild swan (the descendants of tame birds that were introduced into Geneva in 1838), gulls, sea-swallows and numerous birds of passage, such as ducks and divers. There are twenty-one different kinds of fish, the most esteemed of which are the trout and perch. The lake has for centuries been the favorite theme of writers of all countries, among whom are Byron, Voltaire, Rousseau, Alexandre Dumas and others.

Le Pont de Galata

CONSTANTINOPLE.—There is no lovelier scene on earth than that which opens up before the traveler as he approaches Constantinople from the sea, at once so bright, so varied in outline, so rich in color and so gorgeous in architecture. On the left, washed by the waves, the quaint old battlements extend a distance of nearly four miles, and over them rise in picturesque confusion its terraced roofs, domes and minarets. To the right the white mansions, cemeteries and cypress groves run away along the Asiatic shore as far as the eye can reach. In the center is the opening to the Bosphorus, revealing a vista of matchless beauty. Looking northward past the splendid battlements of the palaces and the graceful minarets of the giant mosques, one sees a long reach of the Bosphorus all aglow with palaces, gilded kiosks, villas and terraced gardens; nor is the scene less gay and animated on the water than on land. Huge ironclads lie at anchor within a short distance of the sumptuous palaces. Passenger steamers from every country in Europe are ranged in double rows opposite the docks; corn ships from Odessa or the Danube lie side by side with graceful Greek and Turkish boats, while hundreds of caiques flutter here and there with loads of gold-bedizened beys or veiled women.

127

THE MOSQUE OF ST. SOFIA, CONSTANTINOPLE.—THIS MAGNIFICENT MOSQUE IS CONCEDED BY ALL AUTHORITIES TO BE ONE OF THE MOST WONDERFUL STRUCTURES IN THE WORLD. IT WAS ORIGINALLY BUILT BY THE EMPEROR CONSTANTINE IN 325–'28, on the occasion of removal of the seat of the empire to Byzantium, and is so called, not as is erroneously supposed, to a saint of that name, but to the "Hagia Sophie", "Holy Wisdom"—that is the eternal wisdom of God or the Logos, the second person of the Trinity. The building may be described as a square of three hundred and forty-one feet, forming a Greek cross, and surrounded in the interior by a gallery reserved for women. This gallery is supported by magnificent pillars brought from ancient temples. In the center rises a dome that is supported by two great semi-domes. The height of the dome is one hundred and seventy-five feet. This mosque was destroyed in 404, and re-built in 415. It remained unaltered until the celebrated battle of the factions under Justinian in 532, when it was totally destroyed. The present building is substantially that which was erected by Justinian in expiation of this sacrilege. It occupied nearly seven years in its erection. Ten thousand men are said to have been employed upon it. The material was supplied from every part of the empire, and comprised remains of almost every celebrated temple of ancient paganism.

SOLIS THEATRE, MONTEVIDEO, URUGUAY.—The Teatro Solis is one of the handsomest buildings in the city of Montevideo, and said to be the principal place of amusement on the Rio de la Plata. It is a vast building with a seating capacity for three thousand spectators, and was erected in 1856 at a cost of two hundred and sixty thousand dollars. The central portico is composed of eight tall Corinthian columns, the capitals of which are exquisitely carved. The spacious vestibule, paved in marble, is adorned with six finely sculptured marble columns which support the lobby. The interior of the hall is well proportioned, with high ceilings, good ventilation and acoustic qualitites which are said to be unsurpassed. Like all South American theatres there is a pit, used only by men, and the galleries which are divided into boxes or palcos as they are called. There are five tiers of these supported by light, graceful iron columns, the distances between which define the palcos. The stage is broad and deep and capable of accommodating the most complicated stage setting. On the exterior the marble galleries overlook a park, of the same name as the theatre, beautifully ornamented with choice trees, plants, fountains, statues and flowering shrubs.

BENEATH THIS STONE
REPOSE THE BONES OF TWO THOUSAND ONE HUNDRED AND ELEVEN UNKNOWN SOLDIERS
GATHERED AFTER THE WAR
FROM THE FIELDS OF BULL RUN, AND THE ROUTE TO THE RAPPAHANNOCK.
THEIR REMAINS COULD NOT BE IDENTIFIED, BUT THEIR NAMES AND DEATHS ARE
RECORDED IN THE ARCHIVES OF THEIR COUNTRY; AND ITS GRATEFUL CITIZENS
HONOR THEM AS OF THEIR NOBLE ARMY OF MARTYRS.MAY THEY REST IN PEACE!
SEPTEMBER, A. D. 1866.

ARLINGTON CEMETERY, ARLINGTON, VA.—Just across the Potomac from Washington, D.C., in the National Cemetery stands the here photographed monument to unknown Union soldiers who were killed in the Civil War, erected by and at the expense of the United States government. The site of Arlington Cemetery occupies the grounds of the old homestead of the Lee family, one of the illustrious members of which was General Robert E. Lee of the Confederate army, and one of the greatest of modern commanders. He was born at Stratford, Va., in 1807. His father, General Harry Lee, was well known in the War of Independence as "Light Horse Harry Lee", and was afterward elected Governor of Virginia. When the Mexican War broke out Robert E. Lee was captain in the army under General Scott, and distinguished himself greatly throughout the campaign, being made colonel for his heroism at the siege of Chapultepec. Lee was one of the commanding generals of the Confederate forces during the late Civil War. To do justice to his extraordinary ability as a general under circumstances of extreme difficulty, when his movements were continually hampered by political necessities, as well as by the lack of material resources, it would require an elaborate military biography. His character shone out radiantly noble even in the last stages of that unfortunate struggle.

THE UNITED STATES NAVY YARD, BROOKLYN.—The Brooklyn Navy Yard is the chief naval station of the American republic. It contains forty-five acres and is enclosed by a high brick wall, within which are numerous foundries, workshops and storehouses. Representative vessels of every kind used in the United States navy may usually be seen at the docks undergoing repairs or alterations, as this photgraph shows one of our naval vessels being repaired. The yard has an extensive frontage on the East river and contains a dry dock which is built of granite, the cost of which approached two and one-half million dollars. Although Brooklyn in some measure serves as a suburb for the residents of New York, and many of its inhabitants carry on their business in that city, its own commercial activity is very great. Most of the river frontage is lined with basins, wharves and docks, the most important of which being the Atlantic dock with an area of forty acres; the Erie basin of sixty acres, and the Brooklyn basin of forty acres. Its principal park is Prospect park, which embraces more than six hundred acres. Washington park, another open space in the city, is the site of ancient fortifications. Brooklyn is connected with New York by the well-known Brooklyn bridge. Another bridge is to be constructed, for which the ground was recently broken; it will join the northern part of New York City with another portion of Brooklyn.

HARVARD COLLEGE, CAMBRIDGE, MASS.—There is some diversity of opinion among those who have not attended American colleges as to their respective superiority, but that diversity of opinion does not extend to their students. It is universally admitted that Harvard and Yale are representative of the higher institutions of learning in America, and they are, therefore, included in this volume. Harvard was founded in 1638, at Cambridge, Mass., by a former fellow of the Emanual College at Cambridge, England, and represented the Puritan tenets for which the parent society was at that time noted, from which Puritanical basis there has been, to say the least, some slight relaxation. Harvard men are to be met in all walks of life—the struggle for existence sending those who have opportunities to the top, and those who are unfortunate and without financial assistance to the foot of life's ladder, though, of course, a man whose mind has been trained is much more apt to accomplish lasting results than one who has had but meager opportunities. The cost of a course at Harvard is such as can be regulated to the purse of the scholar, not that there is a sliding scale for pupils, but the student can work and save useless expenditures sufficiently to enable him to pass at a comparitively slight expense.

BRIGHTON BEACH, CONEY ISLAND.—Coney island lies on Long Island's shore just outside the Bay of New York about ten miles from the city, and consists of a very narrow island four and one-half miles long. The island is divided into four parts, most popular of which is the here pictured Brighton beach, it having more complete and extensive opportunities for bathing than other parts of the island. At West Brighton there are two iron piers extending thirteen hundred feet into the ocean, one of which is here photographed. The view from coney island of the Atlantic ocean is charming, it being possible to see ocean steamers sailing in and out gracefully over the bosom of the deep. It is the resort, par excellence, of New York's weary workers, it not being an unusual occurrence that there are one hundred and fifty thousand people visit the place in one day. The means of access being of a very superior nature, and the fare from any point in New York city not exceeding sixty cents, it makes it, perhaps, the most popular resort in America. Roackaway beach had, up to the time that Coney island became so popular, been the favorite resort for New Yorkers. Long Branch and other New Jersy points have great attractions for visitors, thousands of whom go down to these points to spend their summer vacation.

133

CITY HALL SQUARE, NEW YORK.—It is difficult to imagine, when looking at the building in the foreground and seeing beyond it the vast structures which have been erected, that at the time of the City Hall's construction the south front was built of white stone and the City Fathers objected to the expense of the construction of the rear or north front of anything other than brown stone, which was cheaper, urging as a reason therefor that the city would never extend beyond the City Hall and few people would see it, and therefore it was unnecessary to assume the additional expense that would be incurred in substituting white for brown stone at the rear of the building. The City Hall is a pleasing structure in the Italian style, three stories high. It is two hundred and sixteen feet long by one hundred and five feet in depth and adorned by a cupola containing a four dial clock, which is illuminated at night. It was erected during the years extending from 1803 to 1812 at a cost of five hundred thousand dollars and is occupied by various public offices. The governor's room in the second story contains a writing desk on which Washington wrote his first message to congress, the chairs used by the first Congress and the chair in which Washington became inaugurated as president. The Court House, which is just back of the City Hall, is the building which caused the downfall and incarceration of William M. Tweed and his associates.

THE LEVEE AT NEW ORLEANS.—The city of New Orleans is situated on a bend in the Mississippi river some nine miles in length, which forms the harbor, or levee, as here photographed. The river at this point varies from fifteen hundred to three thousand feet in width. Around the margins of this fine harbor a line of steamers and shipping extends for miles on either side, and pictures to the unaccustomed eye a fine sight. The activity of the averge New Orleans levee darky is, as can be imagined from this photograph, of a rather negative character. New Orleans is exceptional among the cities of the United States for the picturesqueness of its older sections, and the language, tastes and customs of a large portion of its people. Here in early days were landed those cargoes of French girls, supplied each with a chest of clothing, and proudly famed long afterward by their numerous descendants as "the girls with trunks." The climate is not marked by extremes of heat or cold; the wide reach of water and wet lands that lie about the city temper the air, and the thermometer rarely passes above ninety-five or below twenty-seven degrees. Those who visit the city between the months of November and June may enjoy the delights and beauties of a redundant springtime, and find easy entrance to the social gaieties of a spirited, pleasure-loving people.

Y ALE COLLEGE.—Was founded in 1701 by the combined action of a few of the ministers of the state, a charter being given in the same year by the Colonial legislature. It was for a long time chiefly supported by the Congregationalists, but is now nonsectarian. In the United States university education has received a great extension, without, however, exercising in Europe that reflex influence discernible in so many other relations. Although higher education has unquestionably been very widely diffused, the undue multiplication of centers has lowered the standard of attainment and led to a consequent depreciation in the value of university degrees. This tendency it was sought to counteract in the State of Ohio, some thirty-five years ago, by an organization of the different colleges. The instruction given is, in most cases, almost gratuitous, the charge to each student being less than thirty dollars a year. The distinguihsing characteristics which belong to these numerous centers are described by the president of the Johns Hopkins University, in an address delivered in 1866, as suggestive of four different classes of colleges: First, those which proceed from the original historic colleges; second, those established in the name of the state; third, those avowedly ecclesiastical; fourth, those founded by private benefactions. To the first class belong Yale and Harvard colleges with their offshoots.

PRINCETON COLLEGE, PRINCETON, N.J.—Princeton college was founded in 1746 by members of the Presbytery of New York. It was chartered in the same year and opened at Elizabeth in 1747, removed to Newark in the same year and finally transferred in 1776 to its present site. Almost all the buildings owned by the college are the gifts of generous benefactors, the most magnificent of whom was Mr. John C. Green, by whom, and by the trustees of his estate, not less than a million and a half of dollars has been given in buildings and endowments. The governor of the state of New Jersey is ex-officio president of the board of trustees, who are twenty-five in number, in addition to the president of the college. The trustees appoint the members of the faculty and have entire control over the funds and property of the college. They fill all vacancies in their own body. In the cemetery, which lies just to the north of the college, are the tombs of John Edwards, Aaron Burr and other eminent men. Princeton is also the seat of the oldest theological seminary of the Presbyterian church in the United States. At Princeton on January 3, 1777, Washington defeated the British forces, and the Continental congress met in the town from June 26th to November 4, 1773.

THE MORMON TEMPLE, SALT LAKE CITY, UTAH.—This building is one of the architectural wonders of America. When its foundation was laid it was necessary to transport the huge blocks of granite of which it is composed, by means of ox teams; and for thirty years such a scene in the streets of Salt Lake City was of every-day occurrence. The temple has but rcently been completed, forty years having been consumed in its erection. The most prominent Mormon was Brigham Young, who died August, 1877, leaving a fortune of $2,000,000 to seventeen wives and fifty-six children. He was succeeded in office by John Taylor, an Englishmen, although the actual leadership fell to George Q. Cannon, "first counselor" to the president, and one of the ablest men in the sect. The year 1877 was otherwise signalized in Mormon history by the trial, conviction and execution of John D. Lee for the Moutain Valley massacre of 1857. Of late years the question of Mormonism has largely occupied public attention. In 1873 Mr. Frelinghuysen introduced a bill severely censuring polygamy, and declaring that the wives of polygamists could claim relief by action for divorce. In 1874 the committee of the House of Representatives reported a bill which reduced Utah to the position of a province, placing the control of affairs in the hands of Federal officials, and practically abolishing polygamy.

CHINATOWN, SAN FRANCISCO.—That individual who visits "Frisco" and not Chinatown is like he that reads a review of a book and feels that he knows the volume thoroughly. That district embraced in a few blocks in the heart of San Francisco, and known as Chinatown, is perhaps as famous a spot as America contains. We doubt if there is a more repulsive, yet more attractive place in this great republic. The Chinese live there in the same manner that they do in the flowery kingdom, retaining apparently the worst of their home traits, and adopting as many bad American ones as they can, with the exception of drunkenness, which lapse of good habit the Chinese are not fond of as a class. They use opium in its place. The here photographed building shows one of their restaurants in the Chinese quarter. Adjoining it are tenements occupied by people that frequently are packed twenty or thirty in a room, some twenty thousand Chinese living here where twenty-five hundred Americans would be crowded. A most peculiar sight is their grocery and meat store. For the sake of economy whole pigs are roasted at once and sales made of roast pork therefrom. The carcass is usually hung outside of the store in the blazing sun and a sort of a varnish coating placed on it. One can imagine the startling effect of such a combination in the sunlight. The Chinese also have their theatres, joss houses and temples, to say nothing of gambling dens and opium joints, which it is well to visit accompanied by a police officer, as they are not only filthy, but dangerous places to visit alone.

THE PONCE DE LEON HOTEL, ST. AUGUSTINE, FLA.—The three most costly structures in the confines of the United States are the National Capitol, the Capitol of the State of New York and the building of the Equitable Life Assurance Society in New York City. These were the result of greater outlay than the group of Flagler hotels here photographed, but in none of them is the power of wealth so omnipresent. Royal palaces are interesting in their way, but to find in St. Augustine these buildings copied from old Spanish and Moorish desgins, erected at a fabulous cost, is almost beyond the comprehension of the fascinated beholder. It is said that one of America's most famous authors on seeing the Ponce de Leon and its outlook on parks and luxurious courts acknowledged his utter inablility to write a description that would adequately describe it. Such being the case the reader can scarcely expect me to here do other than emulate his example. The Astors have paid, for two people, forty dollars per day at this hotel and got the value of their money, too, for it is assuredly the place of all places in America to get absolutely the best that is to be had in every sense of the word. The buildings were erected by H.M. Flagler, the Standard Oil king, as a plaything, certainly not for profit, as his fianances are in such shape as not to require the income from the hotels. The buildings are a poem in colors of red, gray and green.

THE UNITED STATES CAPITAL, WASHINGTON, D.C.–Its public buildings are, of course, the chief attractions to visitors to the city of Washington, and the Capitol is not only the finest of these, but probably the most magnificent public building in the world. It crowns the summit of a hill, which is ninety feet high, thus setting the building off to the very best advantage possible. The Capitol consists of a main building three hundred and twenty-five feet long by one hundred and twenty-one feet in depth with two extensions, each two hundred and thirty-eight by one hundred and forty feet. Its whole legth is seven hundred and fifty-one feet, and the area covered somewhat more than three and one-half acres. The material of the central building is the same as that in the White House, a light yellow freestone, which has been painted white, but the extensions are of pure white marble. The dome over the rotunda in the center of the Capitol is the most imposing feature of the vast pile and is the third largest dome in the world, being exceeded in size only by St. Peter's in Rome and St. Isaac's in St. Petersburg. The cornerstone was laid by Washington in 1792. The building is typical of the majestic country it serves as a capitol. Every American can rejoice at the beauty of their capital city–it being among the finest in the world. The view from this building embraces a picture of unsurpassed beauty.

THE STATE, WAR AND NAVY DEPARTMENTS, WASHINGTON, D.C.—Adjoining the White House is the vast and beautiful building occupied by the State, War and Navy departments, here pictured. It is constructed entirely of granite in the Roman Doric style, four stories in height, three hundred and forty-two feet in width and five hundred and seventy-six feet long, thus forming, with the exception of the Capitol, the largest building in the city of Washington. The State department occupies a large portion of the building, smaller portions being allotted to the War and Navy departments. The hall of the Secretary of State and the Embassadors' salon are probably as fine rooms as there are in the city; the latter expecially being a magnificent apartment. The Washington monument is another of the structures in the city of Washington that command admiration, and prior to the erection of the Eiffel tower in Paris was the highest structure in the world. It was dedicated with appropriate ceremonies on Washington's birthday, 1885. Its design contemplated a shaft six hundred feet in height, but after two hundred and fifty thousand dollars had been expended and a height of one hundred and seventy-four feet reached, funds gave out and the work was suspended. Congress then took the matter in hand and made an appropriation which completed the monument. It is now five hundred and fifty-five feet in height.

THE WHITE HOUSE, WASHINGTON, D.C.—Although best known to Americans as the "White House", the official name of this building is the Executive Mansion. It is constructed of freestone painted white, and is one hundred and seventy feet in length by eighty-six feet in depth, two stories high, with portico at the main entrance supported by eight columns. The cornerstone was laid in 1792. The building was first occupied by President Adams in 1800. It has since been the residence of every president continuously, with the exception of four years after 1814, at which time it was burned by the British and took four years to restore. When one realizes that such presidents as Lincoln and Grant have lived beneath its roof, it is with difficulty that the emotional spirit of Americans can be subdued. The grounds surrounding the building extend to the Potomac and comprise about seventy-five acres, of which twenty are enclosed as the President's private grounds. The east room which is open daily from ten until three, is the grand parlor of the president. It is a fine chamber eighty feet long and forty feet wide and twenty high, finely decorated and furnished. The green, blue and red rooms are on the same floor and are most elegant in their appointment. The executive office and the cabinet room are on the second floor, as are also the private rooms of the executive's family.

143

THE UNITED STATES TREASURY BUILDING, WASHINGTON, D.C.–This magnificent building is another of the public edifices at Washington that astonish and command the admiration of every visitor to our National Capital. It is four hundred and sixty-eight feet in height, two hundred and sixty-four feet wide and three stories high above the basement, and was erected at a cost of six million dollars. The materials used in constructing this building were Virginia freestone and Dix island granite. The building contains about two hundred rooms, the finest of which is the cash room extending through two stories and lined throughout with rich marble. The gold room contains many million of dollars of gold coin, and is to be seen only by special permit from the treasurer. All the notes, bonds, etc., of the United States government are printed by the Bureau of Engraving and Printing, in a building which is a branch of the treasury, and is situated not far from it. The site of Washington, if not chosen by George Washington himself, seems to have been selected directly through his agency, and it was he who laid the corner-stone of the Capitol. It appears to have been Washington's desire that it should be called the "Federal City", but in deference to popular demand, the name of the "City of Washington" was conferred upon it. The best time to see Washington is during the session of Congress, or at a Presidential inauguration.